# Street Hymns to the Disconnected

## Poetry, Lyrics and Film Scripts

### By

### J.D. Glasscock

# This book is dedicated to love

Copyright 2008/JD Glasscock

ISBN # 978-0-578-02751-7

I think about her often.....the softness of her voice when the word "love" escaped her breath....even the crisp strike of timber when her anger slapped the Words "Fuck you Jonathan" into the ethers...sometimes life doesn't always travel the direction we would like.....but I cherish the knowledge I have embraced and tasted love at least once....it is a beautiful world to know....if but even for a moment

# A message to the unwary

**Flip the bones and let them roll the attributory tones of truth assembled in the application of insinuations.....let us carpet the ignorance of generations in the sheepdom of calculated perpetration of Plato's Allegory of Caves twisted into the algorithms of humanity's shallow swimming constructs**

# Prayers are delusions given as safety nets to the broken

Poor people crayon dribble signs for a voice... for healing to the woes of their attrition...yet derision is their boon.....laughter echoing upon their browbeaten limbs.....when did humanity become something you earn...something given as golden tokens for those who play the game....fame...name.....everything seems the same....love is a baton passed to only those who can show riches beyond the dwindling of their morality...mortality creeping upon us in scars written in stars....faith a mortar to a crumbling ideal...honesty a trophy to those who lie the best....hip shot in the trenches of pit fights in the ascendancy of truth...and I shed a tear for the infants force fed the doctrine of shallow swimming...how in the pursuit to conquer sidewalk recognition one should not pay attention to the flesh one presses beneath their heels..it is only a dream drubbing itself in a perpetuity of loss.....becoming smaller and less significant the farther one stumbles in the avenues of their own adoration....my bones crumble in the fall of this precipice

# Jumping the Broad Street

I'm a poet chopping streets
Turning corners
Chewing trails
Smoke seeping from fingers
Pretty pictures in roofs of mouths
Tongue clicking
Ticking

# Chains Forged....Unbending and Unbroken

Crenellations of rats in the foundation of dark weaves obliterating the fruition of love......scum sucking the soil of romance through drugged up rape driven dance....tossing pills in drinks.....tearing the morality of innocence as it tries to speak....the revelations of truth in the ruination of freedom through laced bound bars and honor striven ...from tar....how do these people walk past a mirror in the oil that seeps from their flesh and not see the dissolution of their own humanity? How do people rip hearts from the goodness of others and laugh in hysterical fits of madness likes it's a toddler game of tag? I try to grapple the mud that clings to my spirit and forgive the insanity of my love as she is dragged through the Hollywood glitz of depravity..I try to hold to my own morality as a life line to the vervantly tilting carnival of this trumped up reality.......I try to chain the seething anger and pain that threatens to drown the erratic heart beats thumping a dirge against my chest....try to swallow the vivid visions of love fornicating itself against the pelvis of debris and refuse......refuge in the dwindling faith watching the thread unraveling against the wailings of a soul..........my forgiveness is a calm I place as balm upon my lovers eyes....my limbs wound around her to take the acidic bites of snakes coiling ..within her wake.....we will solicit prayers to fulfill the grace etched in the face of our righteous path.....we will link hearts to send off staccato notes of defiance against the hyenas circling our haven.....we will not bend and we will not break...we will not give the pleasure of our rotting bones to the demons succoring upon our crest fallen misery.....we will stand firm and vibrate truth to shackle the demented falsity of these lip smacking denizens of duplicities altar....they shall fall.....they shall fall...they shall know what it is to be burned by the blessings of Creation's destiny woven in love letters we etch across our skin.....tattooed against the ruminations of all who would threaten to topple the story we penned in fate's weave before our spirits left wombs.....we shall endure the wind tossed storm of their sickening assault and shall give them bright chains of runes spelling love in the fabric of their self immolated tombs.....our world has just begun and yet to be written.....

# Fuck me eyes

I love the way her hips sway against the wind
the way her dress moves like the curves of a river
I love the way her lips say hello
soft kisses in dimly lit beds

She's got some serious fuck me eyes
sensous cuddly pillow talk thighs

I love coming home to her beauty
to her limbs manic in sultry shapes
shaking sweat to radio hits
her hair like strands of the moon

She's got some serious fuck me eyes
sensous cuddly pillow talk thighs

I love the way she wakes me
a gentle whisper slipping off her tongue
her arms snuggling dreams through sheets
husky breaths causing thumps in my chest

She's got some serious fuck me eyes
sensous cuddly pillow talk thighs

I love the memories I hold of her
the scent of dresses in brushing silk
scratched bed posts in remembered flesh
the tip of a song as it tilts the night

She's got some serious fuck me eyes
sensous cuddly pillow talk thighs

I love even the sillouette she casts
as she swayed to goodbye
one turn of her head and small grasp
of her hand and a longing to change the tides

She's got some serious fuck me eyes
sensous cuddly pillow talk thighs

I'll miss her till my heart beats the secret of forever...

## Sly Wily Fellow recites story
## From behind smoking pipe

When I was a small boy
I created worlds in which to dream
Vast empires to conquer
Leaving smoky tales for
Fabled Bards to sing


I had princesses to rescue and love
Gave them pearls, gave them doves
And I did it all within
A room of brown
A room of brown


And within it's shadowy fold
I embraced fantasies and willful woeful Stories
I flew with birds and felt free
Played and danced with the twinkling stars
And the howls of the
Merry sometimes-smiling moon
From within the shadows and the trees


And I went to bed every night
With the scent of flowers
And the soft sound of ocean waves
Lapping up on sandy sultry beaches
And every morning I woke
To the warmth of soothing sunrays softening
My sweat soaked flesh
Tantalizing and teasing the
Glory of a morning's misty breath


And I did it all within
A room of brown
A room of brown
druidic healing crowns
swan lakes of moonlight's merry howling face
branches  reaching with quests
birthed in heaven's graceful gate
a last lonely call to fate

all within a room of brown
a room of brown

and oh yes!!!
Here they come, here they come,
The jokers and the clowns
Sexy white strapped ladies with dainty hankies
And creased weather torn frowns
And then of course the wolves
Slathering and slavering in their belated hunger
Yellow and green dragons
Filling the air with fire's
Forked danger
And Reality!!!!!
The scariest demon of them all

And on that note
Begins the telling of the story
An antiquated story about two lovers
Entwined equally between the freedom of destiny
And the cage of history

The Wolf Knight and his Ferocious Feline
Their movements sending ripples through
The strings of time
A blind man walking the tightrope of rhyme

The world turns
Another chapter

They fought as much as they loved
One liked ravens, the other,
Doves

But oh how they lit up a room
Like the sun at high noon
Or the flowers in the summer when they bloom

It made a storyteller want to cry,
Weep in the wildness
The chaos

Brown rooms and faded ghost friends
Gather to say goodbye
Smoke a joint
And get real fucking high

Wanna talk about this storybook romance
Enmeshed in the tenderness of spirit and flesh

An invitation goes out to
The clowns and the monkeys
The sexy ladies and their flunkies

For now the trip begins
The trip begins

A caravan struggling towards
A jeweled horizon
Holding secret ridden smiles
And worn scarred hands
Left over players from the silent band

And our couple, our couple
Glide up that mountain forest walk
Fight side by side
Then stop under the moonlight
For a little, …talk

The crowd balances on tippy toes
Hoping to catch a glimpse
To the finish of this tale
Their impatience gliding
On the rhythms of their
Hips, smirks and grins

The story dissolves into
Tranquil blue skies
Shaded dreams
Rooms of brown
Clowns with frowns
Gaps between God's teeth

Sly Wily Fellow falls asleep
Pipe still burning,
smoking

# Humbled Shores

archaic stone...aged in years.....cinder blocks incasing heart's fragile
wanderings...she is moon filtering through trees on a clear swept night...she is blues
blistering on a summer eve..jazz overtones tilting smiles..cracking
foundations....breaking cinder....her eyes are ocean in a desert....her lips supple as
petals....her limbs and spirit..wings feathered in grace.....her soulful sound issuing
fragments of fables long ago thought lost...
Freedom is a taste this shriven heart had thought but a memory....a cobblestone
history no longer remembered.....yet within her touch...fingers brushing cobwebs
from stone....the words "I love you" crack the inviolate...ignite a fury of passion
bottled and tossed to swelling waves....a cold churning boy drowning saved...and it is
for this gift she gives with such yearning . such innocent truth...that to her....the
world is rendered in archaic script....from scarred torn lips...a faith and loyalty
blossomed upon her feet in rune carved lumines.....I love her.....till the moon spits
it's dust upon our humbled shores...

## Crossroads in the stream of shadows
### A poem written on the day of my Grandma's funeral

I sit here at the precipice...the crossroads....the meandering of rivers collecting into tears I place in soft gentle moments....my memory of love....in being held.....in whispers to ears of compassion and fierce pride.....in journeys to fall away places....to drifting dreams now long forgotten...to sifting sands...holding castles that should of crumbled a destiny ago....We have but fleeting pinches of God's dust in which to choose a path...in which to choose a breath....in which to rally our spirits to.....it is in these blinks...in these far away yet immediate folds of ethereal nothingness in which to create...to merge...to facilitate a reckoning between our pasts and today......my emotions are a churning maelstrom of identity and sorrow and love and joy and meaning and dreaming and weaving and fate......my eyes are brewing storm......falling sunlight in dappled meadows.......forest echoes........I drift and sleep and awake to immerse in the chapels of old and worn writings.....I pray....that I may walk....that shadows may hide but never blind to that which I must find.....forgiveness, love, forgetfulness, wispy clouds holding secrets and contentment......laughter and fulfillment.......and it is with these accruements I pick up the prayers I adorn my flesh with...travel beyond the stars I bind my spirit with and move past the sins I have chained myself with....freedom, a gift given only to those who choose to let go....my wings are unfurled and lifted to grace, I have tasted the transcendence of my pain and sorrow and regret and shed myself of it's unruly weight. My shadow is a stream at the tumultuous crossroads and I have broken the cage....love is the path I choose to take.

# The Fall of Wonderland

Wonderland has fallen
Alice has lost her name
The White Rabbits broke his clock
The Queen has misplaced her King

Everything falls in time
A misplacement of the rhyme
Not even the Caterpillar's smoke
Can lucidate this moving scene

Wonderland has fallen
Alice has lost her name
The White Rabbits broke his clock
The Queen has gone insane

Everything falls in time
A misplacement of the rhyme
Not even the Caterpillar's opium
Can lucidate this moving dream

The Mad Hatter packs his hat
With chinaware and the March Hare
The Mouse gets left behind

The Chesire Cat all alone
Smiles the whole while
Blinking in and out
Pearly whites
Sharp smile

Must've found a new victim
For his mischief
Must've found an old victim
To create a rift

Another time
Another rhyme

**Alice has lost her name**
**Wonderland has fallen**
**The White Rabbits broke his clock**
**Wonderland has fallen**
**Wonderland has fallen**
**Wonderland has fallen**
**The Queen has misplaced her King**

# The sorrow of death at sunrise

sideway alley kicking dirt in the faces of children.....blues trumpeting glory in the dustpans of history.......she called my name and I hid.........broken promises.....her lips red as furnace......as tips of flame arcing tongues.........she has opened veins in retribution for jazz in the culmination of sorrow.........tears carving passages in the truncation of lullabies served in the degeneration of goodbyes......and the little ones cry.......cry...................gasoline screeches of rubber in the tread of souls.........let us celebrate the way the music rolls.........I have spoken and the sound is dying......mama.....protect me...........my limbs scribe answers I will never understand....forest echoes......sanity are saltines given as gifts.......polly want....hang and fuck the sex away........the melodies are drifting....the sky has broken........we are dead...........

# Songs on the Bayou

My Uncle Stanely used to say
On the hot summer swelters
Of a bayou day
You could feel the love of New Orleans in your veins

It's the way the sweat swings jazz to your step
The strength of it's people and the sorrow they have wept
It's the Sun beating you down till your 6 feet in the ground
And pulling yourself back up till the blues of your loss has filled your cup

Cause this is the story of determination and glory
About a city who wouldn't give in
Drinking their days away on a bottle of gin
Listening to swamp toads tell them where to begin
As the world watches and prays
the world watches and prays

People sitting on hot tin roofs of another man's dreams
Watching the cars and houses float by
The levies spilling over the seams
And everyone's stomach growling lean

But in New Orleans town
The people got hearts that don't lay down
Cause you know in New Orleans town
They pulled together and found their common ground

The crumbled buildings sang their laments
The corpses and children got caught in a rich man's net
But people down south are used to blues spittin from their mouth
And  no way were they letting this back room play get in their way

So they dug deep…scratched what they needed
from the love they had sown and now reaped
and stood tall….a proud man's courage rising from a fall
and laughter and joy were the calling cards called

My Uncle Stanely used to say
On the hot summer swelters
Of a bayou day
You could feel the love of New Orleans in your veins

It's the way the sweat swings jazz to your step
The strength of it's people and the sorrow they have wept
It's the Sun beating you down till your 6 feet in the ground
And pulling yourself back up till the blues of your loss has filled your cup

Cause this is the story of determination and glory
About a city who wouldn't give in
Drinking their days away on a bottle of gin
Listening to swamp toads tell them where to begin
As the world watches and prays
the world watches and prays

People sitting on hot tin roof's of another man's dreams
Watching the cars and houses float by
The levies spilling over the seams
And everyone's stomach growling lean

But in New Orleans town
The people got hearts that don't lay down
Cause you know in New Orleans town
They pulled together and found their common ground

The crumbled buildings sang their laments
The corpses and children got caught in a rich man's net
But people down south are used to blues spittin from their mouth
And  no way were they letting this back room play get in their way

So they dug deep...scratched what they needed
from the love they had sown and now reaped
and stood tall....a proud man's courage rising from a fall
and laughter and joy were the calling cards called

And now sweet sweet New Orleans
Plays it's jazz all night long
In memory of sorrow and courage in song
Let's the blues drink up the bayou smooth
So everyone knows nothing left to prove
We got beauty and laughter and joy
We got children with smiles playing with their toys
And it's a wonderous thing to enjoy

My Uncle Stanely used to say
On the hot summer swelters
Of a bayou day
You could feel the love of New Orleans in your veins

My Uncle Stanely used to say
On the hot summer swelters
Of a bayou day
You could feel the love of New Orleans in your veins
the love of New Orleans in your veins
It's my home and where my hat will always stay..

# Towers, Cards & Symphony

Heart built upon a tower of cards...spluttering....dueces running rampant...one-eyed jacks falling upon wayward swords....Queens and Kings breaking open dirges against the inevitibility of sacrifice....Aces gathering amongst themselves plotiing rebellion....Hearts disappearing against a deluge of Spades.....Diamonds isolating with airs and talks of elitism...Clubs chanting prayers to the coming bloodshed in the crumbling of love....

A minstrel strums these images into a swirling mealstrom of circumstance...how love is a metaphor to opening oneself to a blade slipping beneath notice....to a symphony of sorrow coealescing within the confines of a chest....

Her words draw crayon cave paintings of romance and an embracing of flesh in statuesque tribute to paramours worldwide but her movements...her actual shooting of tongue into the crevice of limbs artfully sculpting acrimony in the stomping of spirits tells another sordid tale.....one of cracked sidewalks and ghost towns holding broken promises as stop signs.....the sillouettes of dreams haunting lonely streets......caterwhauling about the liklelyhood of dissolution within the dead end avenues of holding to belief....

Red lights flash hovels in the wanton brothels of demure eyes hiding shy soulless glides into the treaties of hollow lies.....and the minstrel's strumming chords come to a slow low fading sound....his body leaning desperate and alone....limp and drained against the thin walls of a tumbleweed saloon....empty and irresolute to the charms of a heart , his lids drooping to unheard of incriminations of trust once again measured against the proliferation of lust over the merits of love......

The lights darken upon the town....shadows scrawling their indifferent melodies, the tower of cards long ago traversed to dust on a melancholy wind....and the music... no longer a viable road to relate a symphony that has no meaning nor ever did....a lonley man bereft of hope stares vacantly into the deepening of night....his fingers tapping murals to nothing and noone.....

## Tribulation does a strut,
## Her kiss is sweet

When our hands touch,
It's tentative, vulnerable
Our eyes revealing too much
Peeling back broken bridges
Cracked sidewalks in smoke hazy mirrors
Dark and shadowed places, her face
Fears and tears buried
Protected

Tributes to ancient tribulations
Scars that walk and talk
Past landscapes, flesh
Soul glide ride
Inside of a dream
Broken shells and
Caverned walls that bleed

I speak of beauty
Residual after shoots
of her eyes
forested mountains
mossy ponds licking meadows

I think sometimes
I think too much
Hollow no feel zone
Bleached bones
On beaches of ash
Tumbled words torn
From scar tissued throat

Belief following utterance
Jarbled sound bytes
My teeth crooked
And wayward
Jagged drips of venom
In the split tongue of a snake
Flickering, sensitive

Imparting whispers
From ethereal lips
To material hips

Nervousness is a disease
Something you ingest
In beginning toddler steps
And eyes that are still remembering
Somewhere else

And the words hit hard
Her exhale, breathing, uttering
"Go for it baby,
go for it"

and her shy glide eyes
say it all
trembling hand
smooth talking skin
ancient age in Saturn pout
and I shout
"You are a dream!"
sculptured curves
wondrous stars
soft sincerity, sanity

and her fingers skip down my chest
flick memories into skin
pain into disease

and she whispers
"Go for it baby,
go for it,
it's love"

## Silence is the segue of life

we walk the sands of remembrance.....echo the hunger in eyes disillusioned in belief.....she smiled and the sun rises within the cavernous diatribe of society's faulty design............and the forest is silent.....soft segue into the fantasy of ecstasy.....her thighs are strong flavored meat to the starvation of hard earned street.....small children flipping coins to the back beat of hopeless romance.......we dream....and sleep....and dream.....and wake only to find sorrow as our bed mate..........foundations of serenity in the comforts of serendipity...............her lush lips coursing the curvature of my flesh as sweat beads in the tintilation of broken seas.....all we can ever do is be......be what we were born to be........fate interwoven in the tongues of destiny drooling the artifice of sacrifice......let us bleed....weary down the alleys bouncing teeth cackling the throes of disbelief.....we are falling yet flying and we have seen the limbs circling our future in tiny spirals in dirt strewn semblance of cracked tethers........restraints a crumbling ideal in the face of TV's blinking streaming stories of death in the pale eyes of children.....prayers are the only whispers we hear.............fear in the tears we spend as monetary fulfillment.....let us breathe....let us choose the road we seed.......

# There's a raven upon my shoulder

I'm sitting here thinking about
All the times I've hurt
The times where pain was the only thing
I could taste
How reality bites till teeth lick blood
How reality never plays around
Doesn't know how to
Like when you get to the point where open eyes
See the death of fables
Where you're no longer innocent and able
Where truth becomes a label
You stick on things
To make them real

When the first gentle kiss becomes a feverish
Tongue shoving meat through chafed and cracked lips
Not enough water in the well maybe
Or just maybe couldn't see past the veneer
hadn't learned how to yet
still rosy pink tints to everything

but the first time I saw scars on her tits,
I cried, realized, everything's inflated
A blown out proportion
Of circumstance,
How chances are moments, choices
That slip between the cracks
Eyes diluted with drugs that never had a name,
Never needed one
When heartbeats skip past the opportunity
When they've already turned to a memory
Before your hand can even leave the holster
And how the paint brush your parents paint with
Is just a smile in rewind
The sound of a whip
That licks the air between your breast
And a mother's womb,
How once you're out,
You can never go back,
How the chasm, the cliff edge,

Expands, grows larger,
The years adding wrinkles,
Weakening morals

They say gray hair is a symbol
For wisdom, but what they don't say means more
How it's just stress breaking bones
Jangled nerves to hot tip needles
Extending from brittle veins
When the fable becomes your label
To stick on things
Cause your no longer good at lying,
No reserves left for trying
Even self-immolated death
Requires too much sweat

So I pick up the pieces
The broken bones
The gentle kisses
The dry cracked lips
I wish to atone for
Sink teeth to self exposed flesh
Bite until jaw lines meet
Chew until memories keel over
Till the pain recedes
Like a drug, like a dog's bark
Echoing then fading into hollow eyes,
Soft sad still moments of compromise
To all the merry go-rounds
The santas with beards falling to pillow case stomachs
To it all melting into mists of forget me nots

I suck in hanging gut
Spit out misery
Pick up my chain heavy garments
Move out past it all
Till the shade trails the shadow
Till flits of flaming sun
Have compensated for where the gun has shot
Bullet hole chest
Where the wound has peeled back and
Exposed brittle skeletal remains
Ghost child fire walks
My feet wandering past the silhouettes
The ricochets of burning dreams
The whale song of bitter seas

Till I reach the end of the cuts
The enflamed flesh
Reach over the chasm
The cliff edge
Roar into song heavy wind

"I will not Surrender!!!"
"I will not Surrender!!!'

thin walls,
circling, spiraling
enclosing
chewed over stomach spears
entwining child throat
exiting infant fostered mouth
chunks of pain and misery
jilted pieces of love
emptied out to collapsed scar toughened knees
pooling around heart strings
and whispers to myself, pleading

"Please, no more, please, no more……I've had enough…"

Eyes seeping shut with wisps of once upon a times
And fables that were real way back when
Till the eyes fill with sand
And say

"Go to sleep young child.  Go to sleep and dream."

And I do sleep
I do dream
And I fall
I fall
Till my skin has grown colder
And Ravens rest upon my shoulder

# Jazz in the teeth of night

**Flipping jazz tunes on the teeth of paradise....the sun in the breeze of wind down alleys...... hear the blues man howl off echoed night....... street lamps flickering, dying, trying to impart whispered truths**

**Death is the triumphant scream of accessibility**

## Humming foundations in the seed of dreams, the coursing flesh of death's teeth

I walk small bricked stone.....uneven and shaky in foundation.......I hum small melodies to myself as I wonder at the blindness of people in general...including myself....I stumble only to catch myself on fragile branches treading the path...they snap and cause me to fall....my knees are scraped and bloody...tooth lodged in lip......I lisp words to the freedom of insanity.......birds sing melodically in distant shores....I pick my weariness up and fold into ethereal being.........lost is the flag I carry in retribution for that which we hide.......I am small child....a memory of a forlorn womb......I am brittle bones in the architecture of a tomb.........sing to me......tell me the lullaby that will heal my soul.....I touch sand and trickle into the depth of sea......we are born and we are seed..........we are the product of society's greed....and we bleed...we bleed.....and I can no longer stand...my dreams are broken shells strewn across a ruby beach... I wish death had softer teeth..

# Beauty is a glorious road

Beauty I think describes her best
It could be her eyes or maybe
Her hips,  lips or maybe just
The way her face glows when we touch

I feel like I've known her before,
Another life, another time,
Both of us cupid's whores

When I'm near her I feel fluttery
Inside, similar to a butterfly

When other women flirt with downcast eyes
All it does is make me think
How pale in comparison they are to her star

Maybe this war was lost before
It began, but if so, then let it be so
Lost is not so bad, it's comfortable, forlorn,
Wayward in her eyes, her hips, lips,
Her glowing face, her beauty,
Yes, beauty, I think that describes it best
Two lovers fading into the twilight of the sun out west

# Lollipop

..baby baby I can't wait till u drift softly in my arms, in my arms I bait the breath it takes to take the test of true true love, true true love.......I handle marbles hoping to win u a cupie doll, a cupie doll to take away the pain, sweep away the pain, in the pouring rain, pouring rain, in the pouring rain, lets take the train to tomorrows edge and scream, scream........

# Love Signs in the Dish of Life

Well there's a story..........Pisces don't like to teach..........lovers ......grizzly poet says sand is the chips of reality etched in memory, in small closets we have hid in......in boogie monsters we have penciled.......and the dream...the dream is myriad stars blanketing the night...............showing the consciousness of life.........and we shall spread... cover the shadows with frail stumbling light....wind tossed candles, wax melting shift spray of oceans smiling............we are but movements...songs........whispers..forget and sleep........dream......

live....breathe....and a soul shall free feather limbs dancing spirals in the breath of god....

# Hope and Feathers

a breath.....a trickling of liquid down parched throat.....shifting shade to the paramour of want...to the silvered strings of far away lullabies........we hope.......we cast coins into deep wells and count the heartbeats till the tinkling sound of breaking water echoes to our ears...we pray....listen to the drop of tears bouncing of scar toughened flesh...to the drizzle of rainbows long ago broken...to pots of gold left tarnished in the back woods of fading dreams......wait....intonations....tumbleweeds blowing the vastness of souls left yearning....embrace.....suffocate.....eyes mirroring stars in unadorned splendour.....lisp the words to insanity...yet hold to the too often felt humbling of feet unwashed and divine.....footsteps carrying us to shining episodes in the limelight of our nourished yet frail avenues......we supplicate....we carry visions....our wings spread before our fall..

# Pistol Whips in Alleys Singing the Blues

I'm just wasting time, counting ticks, writing rhymes,
in the corner lit shadows of dive bar digs
eyes shifting between winks and drinks,
sticks rocking balls in side pockets,
Smoke of scars drifting lazily under swinging lamps

My thoughts like curtains of haze
shift complexity in the opening act of plays
curving around exposed thighs,
teeth cracking gutter sighs
breasts slick with the sweat of consummation
sweet flesh gyrating around open flames, crashing waves,
pewters of shit slipping through the painted slit of lips,
pistol whipped, mind cracking
in the blowing steam of shaded dreams,
woozy under the back alleys of things that do not seem,
things blurry in the conquest of carnality,

drink after drink swallowing the proclivity of true thought
while the thump thump thump of a blues tune
sounds in a crowd chattering in mindless poise
home is not something found in this town,
lost amidst the carnival frivolity of Hollywood haze
everybody trying to be somebody, somebody,
as long as it's not themselves

And I skip rocks of trash can lids,
one for everyone of my numerous sins
as I peel a jazz beat off the summer heat
and croon up tempo blues to the loneliness of days

while straddled between thighs I count the bruises left
on the abuse of childhood saddle games,
daddy used to be,
daddy used to be, daddy used to be so good

33

conscious integrity lost in the pillow of faces
blurred from reality, and I beg,
plead, do not tell me your name, do not exhale,
it is easier on everyone if it is inconsequential
easier for you if you search for love in other places
then the vacancies of my eyes,
ghost towns holding father promises broken in the desert heat
as I turn into the covens of sleep
precognitive in it's restless throes,
stolen glances of morpheus tears unshed in the sandy wails
of youth,

loneliness manifest in the tangled
covers licked to the womb that is a tomb
And I repeat myself, teeth clicking teeth, you are not her,
you are not the one, words mumbling, stumbling
from my tongue into the sweet crevice of their wanton pleasure,
never be the one as I lick and I bite and I tease,
testing the balance of penetration, my prick swollen within
their cave, ripping back into the moment of birth, my cock
slamming into the channels of earth, and I plunge, and plunge
my eyes seeping tears in the memory of childhood fears, shedding love from
every limb, humanity from my very own skin
as I hum a back alleys blues under a glorious moon,
pistol hung to crack my death
you are not the one
you will never be the one.

# A piggy stumbling in the desert, panting, gasping, searching for the love of a white furred rabbit

10 days......they crawl away like a snake slithering in the sun, a light drizzle on a summer day......I see u, breathe u, touch u, but u are not there....your lips are what come to me in the midnight blue, when nothing soothes my sleep but u....you are a memory waiting for me to dream......I long for your laughter to run across the contours of my flesh.....so long to count the ticks passing....a desert, my face chafed in the heat....I call for u and ever so faintly hear your whispers, hiding in the thunder, the flashes carving the sky....where are u....lover, my knees ache from the weight of your absence....I stumble, ears stretched for the silhouette of footfalls, eyes straining for a glimpse of your white fur....it's been so long....so long....come to me..

dryad....druid....muse...shed the illusions that separate our joining....I am weak, short of breath, I need the taste of your scent in sweat.....paramour....I hunger for the gliding brush of your fingers kneading my fear into the courage to embrace eternity....explore....devour....my skin, my lust, my shaking spasaming flesh, my lips upon your breast.....suckling, nourishing the memory....womb...ahh I struggle in this tomb.....lover....my throat is parched in the wanting.....your nectar.....blessings......I await and search, I awake & yearn.....my eyes are half lidded & dreaming of u.........

## Eternity's Sleep – Dedicated to Amanda Joy

Pulling petals to make a wreath to the fae.....weaving starlight....drop skipping stones across ripples of water....my hand is archaic rune spilling forth wisdom in dark corners....trembling spirit in the aftermath of brilliance.....I am tomb.....a forlorn memory of a womb....a storyteller telling fables in the shade wrapped prelude of inevitability...I am sleep in the tilting of eyes half lidded....a lucid moment in the pull of eternity......wake me......my limbs are cement striven paint brushes lacking color.....a reap of humanity in the crumbling precipice of ideals....I am strand of filaments seeking purchase...I am...I am.......lost.....mud and a sinner's weeping.....swallowing me.

# Birds & Toads sing beautiful songs

Imagine a world

Where our child is free

singing gloriously

like a bird in a tree


Imagine a world

where worries are distant

and love is insistent

and our future is bright in gold


'cause these are the stories

written in glory

from which our love has grown


For you are the one

I dream of at night

that sends me to sleep

and comforts me tight

So know in sleep

we sleep to dream

the dreams of dreams to dream


For we are the songs

sung in summer

we are the fire

the warmth in winter

and together we brighten the world


For this is the road

where glorious toads

sing us songs of symphony


Where we grow & we learn

and we sit & and we talk

and listen to the birds & their melodies


For imagine a world

where our child is free

singing gloriously

like a bird in a tree

And imagine

a world

where worries are distant

love is insistent

and our future is bright in gold

For this is the story

written in glory

from which our love has grown

# September 11<sup>th</sup>

Hello, I want to be honest, earlier I wrote an email about a show on a day...a day remembered of as sad tidings and anger....I didn't mention it.....I didn't bring it up......TV land sensationalism took that from me, insensitive diatribe of ticks to the register, oil, give me some money, generals, give me some money.....while people die before the revolution of life ,insensitive, visions over and over again, hammering, hammering, crushing my head with commercials stuck on the beds of real people....Where is the touch in things...... I ponder here now of theses thoughts.....I think upon this day....Music playing, words stumbling, like a rhyme, like the love I have for my lover......thousands....screaming......"I want to love, I want to live, don't kill me"....ethers........spiritual nightmares.....justice......corruption, snakes rearing fangs......justice, an ephemeral ideal, honor, insignificant in the daily life of consumerism, not there, individualistic spiritual patriotism, of ones self and all things that breathe and feel....., my lover is 9 hours away and I could be gone, blown like ash on a foggy day, the ring I envision around her finger lost......I am afraid!!! angry!!!! sad!!!!! What is this world......a kaleidoscope of wonderlands, nostradamus megalomania of whatever your holy book condones...people.......they dream. They see birds in trees, children singing gloriously, ocean pounding rock on summer days, What are we, where our are hands, our eyes, our tongues, Blindness is a temporary affect issued in the tampering of truth, lessons in delusion of one's self....... Horns sound, unbound, we our spread for flight, wings majestic in the sunlight.....we see.....we see Tomorrow.....music.....dream

# Soiled beliefs in the ragged teeth of rats

I'm here thinking about the relations of men & women,

how society's fabrication of falsetto veils upon our eyes

leads to the division of people, equality in the comparison of sex

an argument, a diatribe put forth in maestro clarity

by chauvinistic pigs.


Equality is not equality in all things

but balance in composite algorithms of shared boundaries,

opposite stimulations, but in the ensuement of strictures

put upon by history's masculine inception, pathetic patriarchal

simulations of gigantic proportions, we are percolated in our senses

by books written for men by men trying to disseminate origins.


But tell me, where does the mother, the lover, the daughter

fit in this megalomania perpetrated by men.

Where is the womb, the warmth in tears brushed by fingers,

lips maternally given, where is the written word of the intellect

dancing in the back drop of a women's eyes, the ingenuity,

creativity & compassion...........they are strong...

But here we are traveling down the jagged road

of precipice & faulty design, hum drumming

our days away, drifting, stumbling

from the fabric of consolation, drowning

in the back waters of separation, playing

humpty dumpty sat on a wall,

well you know how that story goes


But I tell you,

only we, we in the pushing of will & spirit

against the mediocrity & disillusionment,

only us in the beat of flesh beneath our chests

can reach out, touch, love,

our salvation,

the mother's of our future generations,

for they are strong

& they are beautiful

# Rain Cross, Four Horses to a Trough

My Mama always said
Light a candle at night
And stroll through the wind
Shield it with your right
And spit out your sin

From the north, Death's
Apocalyptic eyes falls
Upon junkie dreams
Street alleyed thugs
Flipping time for easy scores

Abandoned hovels with hopeless hollow
Shells that used to be men once
Upon a time

And T.V. new's reels
Spread his gospel at 5, 6 and 11
Channels switching from hacked up flesh
In wanna be a star crimes
To teenagers with shoot'em up blues

And his decayed teeth push his feral lips
Into what could only be called a grin
And he beckons skeletal dismissal
To his fellow horse siblings
To emerge from their respective
icy lidded
Graves and inspire the dead end trends
of Armageddon to begin

While out of the east Famine
Stretches her incestuous womb
Over the exposed mouths
Of trembling child hopes,
Visions deluged in a non-existent future
With no shadows in which to throw the fated dice
And she smiles wickedly
Listening to prayers and painful
Dirt strewn tears

Thrown against a Heaven
That has closed it's doors

While people who believe birth is divine
Keep adding up the lines
Not caring whether the numbers that
Represent lives ever grow up to see what their made of

Cause there's always another rice paddy
That needs to be
Filled with student protest dreams
And unfed corpses holding
Children's faces,
Aspiration's left unrealized,
Unfulfilled
Born at the wrong time, wrong sex,
Wrong quota

And maggots and rats and crows and vultures
Feast like true divinity
And Famine has taken her turn

While out of the south looms Pestilence's
Pus filled cratered chiseled features
Spreading her infirmed bruised mottled legs
And touching herself with cracked teeth
Tainted moisture gathering for men to feed
Needles extending from holes in veins
High priced call girls blowing
Syphilis dreams

And when they said aid, it's not aid
But aids that copulates future's demise

While her carnival continues to elicit
Her slut fed smile
While she squeezes her sour milked
Crone like breasts
Racing her equine colleagues
Into the contest
For sinful opulence

And from the western realm
War chortles forth and insidious cackle

44

As he sups on richly meat laden table
Throwing chewed over bones to
Pock marked howling dogs
Who once resembled humanity's visage

And the shells keep pounding and pounding
Distant shores
Foreign soldiers holding to
Chemical dreams as trophies to fighting
For home and country
Their lungs hacking up blood speckled freedom
and lied to government trenches
with political barb wire and
economic chess moves

and his scar torn bruised knuckles
continue hitting agendas
while the poor get poorer and
the rich get richer
and it all gets sewn up
on CNN late night
with the bow carefully color coordinated
with the wrapping

and the bullets keep getting cheaper
and cheaper,
easier to get
and the brethren of the horse
have placed their final bet
the beast awakened
seven trumpets sounding
with his forehead stamped
666

And my mama always said
Light a candle at night
And stroll through the wind
Shield it with your right
And spit out the whole world's fucking sin

# The quandaries of love --bane or blessing?

When does love hurt instead of help? Where does caring destroy instead of nourish? Where is the line drawn in dirt to tell the difference? I contemplate these quandaries as I walk....as my heart beats softer....slower....drifting....the woman who holds my love is an alley strewn with drugs deterioating the grip of her mortality.....chipping away the fabric of her morality....and my feet trail the edge of alone.....is this the future I must look upon?? the same as the past I have already stumbled through?....regret is akin to sin wrapped in skin...it is the chains hooked to our own flesh when other's feelings are far away chimes to one's selfish wants....to one's hungers......and my heart beats softer...slower...wanting to stop altogether....and she is falling and my limbs are too frail to catch her.....so I walk.....further down the road.....my dust ridden tracks marking the passage of my lack of will and wealth in which to act....she carries my longing as a banner with which to blind herself to her own dissolution and the lights dim to but shadows.....and I walk and walk and walk.....my steps faltering....body finding grooves in dirt....till my heart slows....softer...softer....slower.....then stops....collapsing.......and the shadows swirl...and all that is left is a pile of scars and a heart that no longer beats....

# Prince Bumpernickle and his Midnight Foray

Scene – Inside of prince's bedroom, the prince in breeches that bulge somewhat and a linen shirt. The door knocks. He jumps off the bed and opens up it just a smidgen, then looks out, and opens it more to hurry in a young beautiful lass dressed in a simple smock. He grabs her to him and starts kissing her neck and cheek fervently but she pushes him slightly away with a coy look.

Peasant woman –"Your highness I be thee honored....and ...ahh I see you received my note...(pushes him away a little more while arching her neck towards him) in good favor.

Prince Bumpernickle – "Ahh yess of course, (more Kissing)ahh, of course I would, you are the talk of the village, (he plays with her long chestnut hair)of course I would agree to meet you and let us say, have some fun.(his hand gliding lower)

Peasant woman (her sliding his hand back up to her hip)" I am honored your highness though why at such an ungodly hour must I meet you( she keeps her hands between them but nuzzles his neck, him going crazy with passion, like a restrained buck). Surely a prince may see anyone he desires at any hour of any day, especially one of your, uhh, your reputation in the romantic endeavors. (she eyes him seductively) I mean your highness, for you and your devilishly good looks I would be honored to have a tryst, but with thy father giving great boons of gold to any that sire your child it would seem your highness could get any woman to meet you here at any time of day.(her hand grasps his butt firmly which shocks him into slight quiescence)

Prince Bumpernickle " yes you hit it on the head, should we say. I already have 7 bastards that my father has had to pay for and certainly he would again if it happened, his reputation and all,but his consternation at having to do so has led him to having me guarded day and night and only now have I gotten the guards away from my romantic...abode, by the promise of free ale and well, free women this very moment in the stables, but they will not tally long, we must hurry.(he leans toward her again)

Peasant woman "Well then we must sire with all speed....."(she pulls her smock over to reveal a see through shift)" let us be at it your highness"(she thrusts towards him her hand darting low only to rap her knuckles and wincing to the sound of her hand hitting metal)"Sire?!!! Owww, what dust thy hide within thy breeches!!!

47

Prince Bumpernickle—(He looks completely embarrassed)"well, you see, that might be another problem"(He takes off his breeches to show a giant locked metal codpiece.) My last 2 illegitimate children, he had guards around me, so now he, well he tried another course. He had the royal blacksmith reshape a female's, what do you call it.

Peasant woman – (looking determined but daunted)"Chastity belt?"

Prince Bumpernickle "Yes that's the very thing(he raps on his codpiece)I can't even bring myself to say it. Yes he had it fitted for a man, for me and now, its been 6 months, I must find a way(he leans into her smacking her with cod piece she falls back but still determined)We!!!....must find a way!"

Peasant woman – (She clings to him her hand scraping against the metal seeking an opening) "Your highness, we will, maybe you could just slip it out the side...I mean , I've heard the legendary size of your highness by some of your... prior...ahh trysts"

Prince Bumpernickle – (he looks again embarrassed "Well maybe we could, maybe we could.....well, iiffff......if the rumors were actually true...I am afraid they may have been a little overstated."

The peasent woman –(Starting to appear alarmed) – Well but your highness, all of them say it, even the old spinster woman on the hill, the one, well you,  I mean even she said you were hung like the greatest stallion( a look of hope to any truth)

Prince Bumpernickle – "well of course they did, my father paid them good money to!  You know his reputation and all"

Peasant woman – (Her greed still glinting in her eye, her families hopes that she produce a  bastard)but well highness, it's ok, they couldn't be that overexaggerated, im sure if even average size, we could still pull it out, it seems very snug to your skin...hmm but still if even average we could get it out, just enough your highness....."(She hugs herself to  him)

Prince Bumpernickle – (he leans back away from her)"well om... to be perfectly honest....uhmmm, (says it very fast)I'm a little smaller the usual, well, a lot smaller then usual. (Loud and overbearing of the previous words)"I have a solution I borrowed from the blacksmith"(he runs behind the bed and pulls out a hammer and a chisel"here here we could get it off with these.  I've prepared myself for the necessary pain involved in a slight tapping of the ole codpiece"

Peasant woman –(looks shocked then greed blinds her mind)" ahh yes your highness we shall be at it right away"  (she gathers him to the bed lays him down and grabs the hammer and chisel to lock)"your highness just a little tap tap and you shall be free and wweee can,,, well we can......just a tap tap"

Prince Bumpernickle—(A look at relief for final carnal freedom as he gazes through her see through smock)"yes a little tap tap, I think I could handle that… a tap tap, tap away"

Peasant woman—(she begins tapping gently then after nothing a little harder)"just a tap tap"(harder)"tap! Tap!(HARDER) "Sire I think I've got it, it's almost coming(Entire time prince is escalating into groans and screams of "Owww, OW, Your killing me, Stop, Stop")"no were almost there sire just bare with the pain, like a great ocean, coming in(Harder, harder)  Like a great pealing bell of pleasure, here we go, just a little harder(the prince jumps back against the bed frame)

Prince Bumpernickle –"No, no! That's quite enough I think we should try another time, I need bed rest and all, you know, keep those devilishly handsome looks going."

Peasant woman ---(digs into his thighs dropping the hammer and chisel)"No your highness, we will not give up, your carnal freedom and my luxurious prize is awaiting, we will stay on course, stay the road,  drive it until our shrieks of pleasure come together in the bliss of our flesh  in a cascade of primal lust!"(as she's saying this she is moving to the wall where various weapon stands are and she reaches it and says primal lust, she turns with a battle axe in her hand, one last look of shocked rabbit fear in the princes eyes, then move of shot to outside of castle walls a few feet below the window of the princes bedroom seeing the rooms torchlight casting shadows)

Prince Bumpernickle –"No,no,no,no!  No really …..another time(clang)no please stop(clang)No really"

Peasant woman –"no your highness the axe is working I'm starting to see dents" (Clang, clang, clang)"Oh damn,hmmm, need something bigger"

Prince Bumpernickle –"No, not the halberd…..no………."

Peasant woman ---"your going to love it sire, I promise. I will thrust upon you and thrust upon you until you cannot move!"(Giant Clang)

(The camera shifts in a steady movement away and sinking down from lit window and towards mossy woods a hundered yards away to the fading sounds of painful "yowlps" to promises of "riding hard like a great stallion, I mean of course I should be on top your majesty"  (till where the camera rests at ground level listening to the nighttime songs of crickets)

# Taken from above

I remember the night
I was taken up in the bright lights
And the sights I was shown
Let me tell you

It started on a moon spoon spun walk
Deep within the Rustling leaves
Of free feeling forest trail
An escape from the city and it's insanity
It's incessant wail
Running from the raving road warriors
And their immoral lunacy
The bootlickers in their high school click mentality
Trying to hide in a mother's warm womb
Primal elements in their rough wind
Watered laced embrace

So I did it
Went on isolated fire foray
Deep dark silhouetted wilderness jaunt
Just me and the leaves
Me and the furry friendly animal brethren
The soft chirp of avian haven

And then when serenity
Had settled itself into aching abused flesh
Calmness into battered bruised soul
It happened under contemplative sky
Star silvered lucid acid fry

I was taken
Kidnapped
Like a small child in a park
I was hoisted by blinding light
So bright I lost my sight
So filled with fright
I had no fight
Weak as a kitten
Wrapped so tight
Wrong fit better then right
And this is what I saw

I was strapped to metallic hard smooth surface
Ankles, wrists, throat, chest
And waist
I was so scared
My desert dusted mouth
Held a bitter taste
And then it came
The prodding and the poking
Robotic limbs stripped of flesh
Whirling and swirling in jointed jerky movement
Poking and prodding in places
I didn't even know I had places

But it didn't altogether feel uncomfortable
It rode the line between pleasure and pain
Like a hollow tube off a curl lip
In a break shore ride
Like a blood pumping lunar leering
Heroin high
With the downside sticking
sweet sadness inside the madness

Then like a Polaroid flash
When your eyes have spoken past
I saw them as I lay there
Bare to all they could do
Would do, Should do
They showed themselves
Sleek like mercury
Sturdy like steel
Beauty in the canines
Protruding from luscious lips
Sexiness in the cartoon curvatures
Of their thighs
The ballooning voluptuousness
Of their breasts
And the sultriness down low
Glistening sweat

And they made me salivate
Aroused me like a bullet shooting a barrel
A clown painting a smile
A back licking a whip

But this is where it turns hazy
Where my memory chews holes
Sucks the shadowed veins

But I'll have to say
the image that tongue licked lipped my eye
In that final snapshot
That flurry in fortuitous visionary view
Leaves no question
No stone unturned
I had a doozy of a time

And when my eyes snapped open
I saw déjà vu leaves rustling
Moon spoon spun creek bed bustling

And I knew I had experienced the unmentionable
Tasted the unforgettable
And I would never see it again

I walked funny
I walked funny
For two weeks to the day
And every night went to bed
With a big fat grin

# Two Lovers and Two Worlds

This is about two lovers
caught between two worlds
one, a poor man's blues
the other, a woman
in a Hollywood ball room dance

The story was stacked
no room for an empty pocket poet
in this girl's star dusted path
their love destined to fall
sleepy fables on wrong set tables
no matter the heart that held them in thrall

Not even the breath of a kiss
flesh entwined in fate's shaking limbs
could save the breaking of this love
Too many green bills in Beverly Hills
licking their lips to hustle her
as the next big dream hit
to not have movie licked thugs
giving him a shove

So they tell him

"Get your poor poet grubs
out of this star tricked garden
get back to the garbage tracks
you belong
Ain't no room in this Celebrity street
for people like you who beg to eat
where the money is honey
and the brokers are finding you funny
Flipping your protests about love

We got bloodlines to keep clean
in Bollywood carpets roped in red
where we sell the falsity of dreams"

So the poor poet boy
with empty pockets
and a closed tear stained locket
flips lonely lullabies
to the dark shadowed skies

As the Hollywood pimp machine
pumps drug induced nightmares down his lover's veins
all the easier to get her to play the game
as she drunkenly staggers down the bright lit lanes

And the poor man wanders back to the garbage tracks
Scufflin' his feet humming a beat
To the question why
Is love not enough in this world
where debauchery and lust and all that we trust
is sold on corners for pennies and dimes

And the girl in the drug dug daze
Thinks of her poet in so many ways
As the cameras flash bright and red roped carpets
close in tight and she wonders
when will it all go away
Never is forever the men in suits say

This is about two lovers
caught between two worlds
one, a poor man's blues
the other, a woman
in a Hollywood ball room dance

The story was stacked
no room for an empty pocket poet
in this girl's star dusted path
their love destined to fall
sleepy fables on wrong set tables
no matter the heart that held them in thrall

Not even the breath of a kiss
flesh entwined in fate's shaking limbs
could save the breaking of this love
Too many green bills in Beverly Hills
licking their lips to hustle her
as the next big dream hit
to not have movie licked thugs
giving him a shove

So they tell him

"Get your poor poet grubs
out of this star tricked garden
get back to the garbage tracks

54

you belong
Ain't no room in this Celebrity street
for people like you who beg to eat
where the money is honey
and the brokers are finding you funny
Flipping your protests about love

We got bloodlines to keep clean
in Bollywood carpets roped in red
where we sell the falsity of dreams"

So the poor poet boy
with empty pockets
and a closed tear stained locket
flips lonely lullabies
to the dark shadowed skies

As the Hollywood pimp machine
pumps drug induced nightmares down his lover's veins
all the easier to get her to play the game
as she drunkenly staggers down the bright lit lanes

And the poor man wanders back to the garbage tracks
Scufflin' his feet humming a beat
To the question why
Is love not enough in this world
where debauchery and lust and all that we trust
is sold on corners for pennies and dimes

And the girl in the drug dug daze
Thinks of her poet in so many ways
As the cameras flash bright and red roped carpets
close in tight and she wonders
when will it all go away
Never is forever the men in suits say
Never is forever the men in suits say
Love is a commodity that lost it's market
A long time ago in a far away place.

# A dissertation on the state of being

**May the forest be with you......**

In my contemplation of the state of spiritual growth and ideology of humanity I have been led to the following assertations. I see a direct correlation between the scientific boom and corporation of our religious doctrine to the declining health of our spiritual identity and cognizance, as opposed to the false surface lip movement of current popular belief or religious practice. I see a determined movement to the oscillation and dissemination of our children to isometric patterns of belief as in a blind mans bluff....in other words Plato's 'Allegory of the caves' is a direct example of the current functioning of society.....Our sheepish willingness to be led to the point of a deadness of being or in other words no true spiritual connection to any form of womb or naturalistic province of belief....

When as a friend puts it, we start using synthetic chemicals for the everyday answer to our physiological or spiritual problems as opposed to the natural affinities provided by nature we are consciously or unconsciously how ever you will it making bold statements to the future, to the children who follow by example.....We continue to build stone houses with which to huddle our heads in the sand metaphorically and institutionally as opposed to teaching and traveling into the woods from which our birth was brought......we continue to build technology at a rapid rate but do not balance our spiritual growth as to provide a fulcrum, indeed we march upon the precipice of death and do not perceive the threat.....In all things balance must be maintained otherwise you eventually have a dissolution of structure....Yet we continue to plod upon this course as TV evangelists provide blow by blow theatrics and a false sense of spiritual identity while their corporate aims and justifications grow on a global network of vacuuming spiritual aesthetics.....where is the true worship of our animal ancestry, our inner state of true ideology, not based upon force fed doctrine but true inspirations gained by careful thought and heartfelt practice....where do we go when our children would rather contemplate the drones of TVs spelling words, carving picks to flip, than study the philosophy of life and heartfelt blessings of generosity....I know these are assertations, opinions of my own perception and I have no answers, no solutions swimming in the cavernous halls of my soul, but the future as I see it is bleak no matter the roses they spew upon it, I smell the shit beneath the fragrance and I am frightened, angered....This system of war and the counting of coins must somehow end, must find within itself a fulcrum of mediation and meditation, must allow and teach our children the true situation of our spiritual assassination......must give them the opportunity to embrace the forest and all natural affinities found there......these are my thoughts, my avenue in with

,

**which I aim to provide true freedom, the only freedom anyone can ever have, spiritual belief in the solidity of natural preservation and the spirits that form the ethers of our tied fabrics, my children, your children, our children, I hope some day, things change.....**

# Love is like a swing

Love is like a swing

on a summer breeze

moving gently side to side

as we walk in the moonlight

under the stars

gazing in each other's eyes


'cause your the dream of dreams to dream

I think you know what I mean

your the dream of dreams to dream

let me show you what I've seen


Your the one I've waited for

groovin on this circus ride

your my wings, my feathered hope

hope we never say goodbye

'cause your the dream of dreams to dream

I think you know what I mean

your the dream of dreams to dream

let me show you what I've seen


A thousand years upon a thousand lives

my heart shall always press your lips

our faith in fate fulfills to satiate

let me hold you as we make the trip


Love is like a swing

on a summer breeze

moving gently side to side

as we walk in the moonlight

under the stars

gazing in each other's eyes

# Her wings were as beautiful as the moon

My feet travel worn grooves of dirt

contemplate signs

exits


Her smell sticks in my sweat

forms ethereal art

in the shape of feathers


The music drifts......

My words become clumsy & slow

exhale of breath


She is free,


I shade my eyes into the gray

watch as her wings carry her

upon thermal winds


She is free

She is dreaming visions

fairys tranquil, drunk on berry wine,

Festivities

closing upon sleep


They know...

circles within circles

wheel of time grinding

turning

woven in the small patterns

of fate


tears echo the sound of my footfall

teeth tilting true smile

My eyes......

deep, purple blue, stars in the night


"goodbye bunny"

# To Sail the Seas of Broken Dreams

**A short film by JD Glasscock**

**Scene – Daytime – Renaissance period**

**Noble Lady on her knees, two white roses clenched in her hand in front of gravestone.**

Delialeh –(her hand caresses head stone) "I know it wasn't you my brother, I know it was them, her, it wasn't you, never you. As soon as our father died, our, our step-mother, that, that harridan, stuck me in that, that place. Oh Geoffrey, oh, I know you railed against them, I know you fought tooth and nail to stop them, but you were too young, too too young. The years,  ahh, I spent, in that pit.....But when, when you got older, and you were made heir, I thought, I thought you would,, would get me out  of that place. They kept me chained, chained like a dog(her eyes become burning embers)  But she must of stopped you, somehow, poisoned you, like, like she took your life (she hugs gravestone) Oh my  brother!!!!!!  Then you, you died, I didn't believe them when they said you were sick!!  I know it was her, them, all her hangers on, her lovers, they poisoned you, put something in your food!!  I know you would never leave me out of choice!!( She leans back and stares hard, fervently into grave stone)  But they will all get their just reward my dear brother!  When you died, you left me everything and they had to, had to let me out.  And now, now, I'm the one they fawn over with their sweet sick lies.   But I have a plan dear brother. Tonight I have invited all of them, all those that sought to bring us down!  I told them I am having a wake for you my brother.  They will all be there, her and her crows, and while I ring in a toast to your life, the servants shall be boarding the doors and windows and as they savor what they think my ears long to hear, my loyal retainers shall light the fire(she squeezes the two roses till blood seeps from her palms onto the white petals) And then, when their death rings upon their ears, embers writing sins upon their flesh,  they shall know, in the hell of their death, they shall know, they shall know!!!  We were Gods amongst a flock of sheep!!!!!"(fade into her eyes, flames dancing in their center until all that fills the screen is flames)

# Mary's Candle

She was a child in a different life
Now she's an angel with soulless eyes
She was a child in a different light
Now she's a victim, a siren in the night

Her name was Mary
She had a hard hard life
Her daddy beat her
Secretly abused her
Almost every night
She cried herself to sleep
Almost every night
Tears on her cheek
Almost every night

She was a lonely girl in the city
She thought she was ugly
When in truth
She was pretty
She was a lonely girl in the city

She was a child in a different life
Now she's an angel with soulless eyes
She was a child in a different light
Now she's a victim, a siren in the night

Somebody light Mary's candle
Somebody show her the way
Somebody light Mary's candle
Somebody help her escape

Her name was Mary
She had a hard hard life
Her daddy beat her
Secretly abused her
Almost every night
She cried herself to sleep
Almost every night
Tears on her cheek
Almost every night

Somebody light Mary's candle
Somebody show her the way
Somebody light Mary's candle
Somebody help her escape

Somebody light Mary's candle
She's just a lost little girl
Somebody light Mary's candle
It could be you in a different world

# Stealin the stolen that was recovered as dreams of one

I'm flipping a top hat pulling bunnies

I got toddler toes scuffling jazz

like the moon in wisps

playing off fingers


I mean I'm shaking it like

a jitterbug popping a tin can

Streets pandering to the flight of birds

chords of music fluttering

my ears like two tons of steer


I got forest in the shanky dank

dive in the back porch

of my dreams

I like wearing baggy jeans

freedom in the drawers

if you know what I mean

It's where I keep my bunnies

white tip fur coddling

the insecuritys

swinging doors to the viability

of my history,

scars the road map to my destiny

as I realize the inescapability

of her eyes

feathered gold in the bones of the sun

# Winter Sleep

Take a ride to the land inside

inside of your mind

where the summers set

and the winters sleep tonight


Take a ride to the land inside

inside of your mind

where the sinners wake

and the infants dream to hide


I've fallen to a place

where mice are afraid

and movies are made

and the criminals are insane


I've fallen to a place

where names are misplaced

in the suffering of grace

and the teeth of humanity's rape

Take a ride to the land inside

inside of your mind

where the summers set

and the winters sleep tonight


Take a ride to the land inside

inside of your mind

where the sinners wake

and the infants dream to hide


I've fallen to a place

of lies & disgrace

in a nation based

on a junkies taste


I've fallen to a place

of memory's face

where rumors are riddles

in the teeth of humanity's hate

Their Hate!!!!!!!

Take a ride to the land inside

inside of your mind

where the summers set

and the winter's sleep tonight


Take a ride to the land inside

inside of your mind

where the sinners wake

and the infants dream to hide

TO HIDE!!!!!

TO HIDE!!!!!

# A Voracious Wolf and Three Degenerate Piggies

A short film
By
JD Glasscock

Scene – A young man coming upon the door to his apartment seeing a big eviction notice on the door, a look of disgust then him entering.  He enters apartment that is dirty and disheveled.  He walks down hallway where 3 doors resides holding crumbled eviction notice he knocks on first door where smoke is wafting from under door.

Dick---"Hey Joe, man I need the rent, we have another eviction notice, Mr. Ludowski is goona kick us if I don't get it to him"

From behind door large amounts of coughing.

Joe – "Oh, man, damn, forgot about that, wow, oh…..well you see man,  I needed inspiration man, gotta drive the beast man, you know, trying to make it as a cartoonist, need the muse man, and a guy had a deal on an ounce of Northern Lights man, so, you know, needed to do it man, gotta feed the dream"

Dick—(looking disgusted) " Joe, you work at a comic book shop, you flunked out of art school and noone is going to buy your stoned out drawings.  I need the money."

Joe—(more coughing)"Well, man I Can't help you, he had a deal that if you bought 2 ounces you got 50 off, so I bought 4 ,uhhh, I mean , 2 and you know, man the bong is my muse, and the muse isn't happy if I don't keep it fed. So you know I had to buy the 4 zzzz's I mean 2 zzz's  ahh yea, but ill get it 4 ya man, you know me……(cough, cough)but I gots to go brother, the dream is calling(Water gurgle water gurgle)

Dick—(Dick kicks the wall then moves down to the next door and knocks on it, a large cacophony of sound)"Hey Marty, hey man, we gots to have the rent we have an eviction notice, Mr. Ludowski said he isn't gonna take it late anymore"

Marty—(Loud belch)"You knows myseeee goods man, I woulds, really wwwwwoddsa help yous, but been having troublesssss again with my girl joooaansss, we got in a major   throwwws down and so I wents and boghtttts a bottle of jack and a 3 small pony kegs, I mean 1 small pony keg, yea, and only 3 bottles of jack, I mean 1  bottle, and yea, im kinda toasted, you know how it is, women bud, women!"

Dick—"C'mon Marty, you and Joan are always fighting and your always getting drunk, cmon man I need the money, Mr Ludowski is gonna make me come over again and give him that full body rub like last month, I had nightmares about it for a week."

(dick hears snoring now from room)

Dick –"Marty…..Marty!!! Damn passed out again"(he moves out into living room and picks up phone and dials)

Dick—"Yea Mr. Ludowski, yea it's me, uh yea Dick, yea MR. Ludowski, I know the rent's late,  yyea, I know it happens every month…….but my roomies don't have the rent……..I mean……no….no……..yea……I can get it for you….uuuh,,, do I have my portion of rent,uhh……well…..you seeee they had this new collection of porn, Ladies Under Moonlight Spread Eagle against the Sky,  I had to have so I bought all 3 copies, I mean 1 copy, wel,,, ahh, you know how it is…….uhh, yea, uhmm, yea, uhh, yes Mr. Ludowski I'll be there, uhhh yes sir, I know the oil you like, lavender scented………ok sir, see you soon……uhh, really, sir the leotard, sir, really….ok. sir…."


(Dick goes to the closet and pulls out a leotard and a bottle of rubbing oil, gives a big sigh like his life is over and heads out the door.)

71

# Aunt Joanne

If Aunt Joanne was a rock star

shed change the world we know

If Aunt Joanne was a rock star

it would be a crazy fucking show


When Aunt Joanne was a little girl

she lived in a fanciful world

she played with her dolls

all night long

Barbie & Ken

she had them do it do it do it do it

do it again and again


If Aunt Joanne was a rock star

shed change the world we know

If Aunt Joanne was a rock star

itd be a crazy fucking show

So when Aunt Joanne hit her teenage years

she felt all alone

she didn't relate to anyone

she thought " Its a fucked up world"

but then she started writing her fanciful songs

about her dreamy world

about Barbie & Ken doin it again

doin it all night long


If Aunt Joanne was a rock star

shed change the world we know

If Aunt Joanne was a rock star

It'd be a crazy fucking show


So then Aunt Joannne spun her middle years

in malibu beach out west

courtesy of her radio songs

and her pink pink pink corvette

yet she still sings her raunchy tales

to make the children laugh

cause she's always known where humor lies

down deep in insanity's lap

so she twiddles her thumb and sings her songs

and lets the laughter ring

while Barbie & Ken do it again

and make the fucking scene


If Aunt Joanne was a rock star

shed save the world we know

If Aunt Joanne was a rock star

It'd be the best damn fucking show

# Doors are sometimes seen through eyes unaccustomed to bright lights

As dreams exit through a window
I find myself within a solitary limbo
Of closed doors and women
In supplication praying for more


My flesh irresolute, chaste in the taste of love,
Doves spreading wings in cloven flight
Against the sky, they are so pretty,
But do not ask me why


Sometimes late at night under candlelight
I slip slide on the verge of lies
Tears filling my eyes till I choke


Could be the smoke wafting in green shades
Across ceilings, gives me these feelings,
About shapes, about curves,
How they linger, fill my scent,
Heave pleasure upon my bones
Show me a golden road


A friendship so bold it deserves to be told,
And her glorious eyes say it all
Make me happy my tongue still clings
To breath, that I have staved off death


And for at least one moment in time
Know love without the complications
Of flesh

# Freedom & love are two distinct possibilities in the winged form of flight

You say you want to be free

you want to see

what's out there

While I sit here

thinking of the things I could say

strumming back alley blues

in the covenant of day


You said love was a gentle flame

warming the halls of eternity

but in the first swallow of rain

your running to the break of history


(instrumental)


I sit here

thinking of the things I could say

strumming back alley blues

in the covenant of day


And here comes the rain

here comes the rain

the part where you run away

here comes the rain

to see what you see

to be as you say free


(instrumental)


Feathered flight in the form of love

it takes two to walk the road

you say I push while you shove

I feel like a swamp in the croakings of a toad


(instrumental)

You say you want to be free

you want to see

what's out there

While I sit here

thinkin of the things I could say

strumming back alley blues

in the covenant of day


And here comes the rain

here comes the rain

the part where you run away

here comes the rain

to see what you see

to be as you say free


(instrumental)


Feathered flight in the form of love

it takes two to walk the road

you say I push while you shove

I feel like a swamp in the croakings of a toad

(instrumental)


And here comes the rain

here comes the rain

So I think I'll catch you later

continue along the way

'cause I hear the music playing

a fast melodic beat

and when it comes down to it

I'm just a back alley dog in a blues dream

a back alley dog (howl)

a back alley dog (howl)

a back alley dog (howl)


And here comes the rain

here comes the rain

here comes the rain

here comes the rain

# Mr. McDougal's Big Day

**Scene -  A small apartment, an old man prepping himself, preening, very meticulously, eyebrow plucking, nose trimming, the whole works as the voice over plays.**

**Voice over – "Little does Mr. McDougal know that this day of all days was going to be a big day> every Wednesday as today surely was, for 10 years, he has gone to the Magical Emporium, where incidentally, you can find all your every day needs, but hold, back, ihh, again to Mr. McDougal.  Every Wednesday since the doors of the Magical Emporium had opened, Mr. McDougal, primps and preens himself, then journeys down to the Magical Emporium.  He never buys anything, but always, and let me emphasize, always has every clerk in the store running to and fro bringing him things for his inspection while he thinks about buying something, which, again, he has never done.  But unbeknownst to Mr. McDougal today would be a different day>  For the employees have gotten together and demanded that the store manager, Thor Odinson, put a stop to the madness that is Mr. McDougal, and bring the employees of the Magical Emporium, where again, you can find all of your every day needs, back to the normal existence, one, without, Mr. McDougal.**

**Scene- shows Mr. McDougal with on last straightening grabbing his hat and cane and exiting the apartment.**

**SCENE – Inside of Magical Emporium.  4 employees gather around store manager as 1 employee enters front door out of breath and ancy.**

**Employee 1 – "ok, the old geezer's coming, he just parked"**

**Employee 2 – "Ok, Mr Odinson, you promised you'd put an end to it today.**

**Employee 3 – "Yes please, I love my job but I'll quit if you don't do something"**

**Employee 4 –"yea you promised, no more"**

**Employee 5 – "No more Mr. McDougal"**

**All Employees – "No more Mr. McDougal"**

**Thor Odinson raises his hands for silence**

Thor – "Yes, yes, everyone to their places, I have it all planned, I wont even give him a chance to speak."

Scene – All employees go to man their respective sections. The door opens and Mr. McDougal walks in. Thor Odinson steps towards him. Mr. McDougal before Thor can begin to speak hands him his cane and hat and strolls right past him to employee 1 sitting at the customer service desk fidgeting.

Thor Odinson – " Mr. McDougal, hold there sir, I really must speak to you, their have been complaints….

Mr. McDougal -- "I can imagine so young man, I would complain to if the store manager interfered with one of my patrons seeking to buy something, now on with ya laddie, I'm gonna have some of these wonderful employees fetch e a few things for my perusal"

(Thor stutters and stammers

Thor Odinson – "No sir you don't, don't, don't understand, I really must speak with you….the…"

Mr. Mcdougal waves him off

Mr. McDougal --- "I perfectly understand, understand that again your wasting my valuable time that I could be shopping. Do you understand that you're here on this God given Earth cause of my sacrifice, that you have your life and freedom because of my courage and daring. I was in two wars sonny, two, and because of my bravery and intelligent action in those wars you sit here today alive and free. I mean young man, really, I took a wound for you and your generation, right here (He turns around and grabs his butt for emphasis) right here, can you imagine, right in my soft spot, and for what, do I tell you, for what, to be bothered and harassed when I could be having numerous things brought out for my possible purchase. Now be a good young respectful man and go get me one of those magical broom sweepers and a top of the line Isis Juicer, and yes the Loki storage wax, there, ye there on that top shelf. Ok hop to it I have a whole list 8 pages long of things I need to look at"

Thor Odinson sighs and gasps and gives up and waves to the employees to be about helping him as he slowly retreats shoulders slumped and Mr McDougal waves his arms imperiously here and there directing the employees on another big Wednesday.

Voice Over – " I cant believe this crap the old man did it again, are you kidding me, this is got to be a joke,….wait ,what, what did you say, ahhh ,, the mic's on, oh why didn't you say so…..ahh, uhmmm, well it seems to be that Mr. McDougal will go on as usual for another 10 years here at the Magical Emporium, where I might add you will find all your every day needs, oh forget this, I quit!!, no, I can to quit, yes, I can too, it's in my contract. I don't care one whit if im some ephemeral voice, I can quit just like anybody else…can to, you can talk to my union representative……I'll sue"

# Steps behind the forefront of complexity

Commemorate the awakening of silence,

the demure eyelids of generations mired

in salient solution,


Tap tap tap, the cane raps sequence

to the direction of blind hovels,

havens to the insincerity of greed

shrunk rapped in the primal ideals

of infidelity, commercial concepts

written in discarded papers balancing

the fulcrum of stupidity......and we.....

we.....we travel the kaleidoscope of

our miseries playing to the back drop

in the lucidities of our realities.....

and we dream......what is dream....

frog paddlin in swamps......knee trudged

footsteps in mud.......we sup liquor

in the delusion of quenched thirst...

cigarettes choke tarring the cobblestones

of our steps.....what is dream?.....


is it in the moments of troubled sleep....

or is it true freedom in the flight of

our fate.....and where does god get in....

in crumbled statues to the burning lay

of platinum, diamond studded crosses....


is it heroes calling upon god as they

finger gold chains & flashes of green

etched in rotten teeth......is it the story

told by a beggar wishing for death or is it

the preacher in stretched limo lamenting the loss of children.....

what is dream........where does god fit in the

scheme of things.......I back pedal musings

in the silence of echoes, melodies quipping quick rhythms

to the benevolence of pale faces treading the bones

of fading halls, frames of superstition in

the attrition of humanity lost.....and we dream....

and we question.....and we believe....and we fall...

and we break....and we bleed...and we wonder....

what does 'it' mean

# Walking in the closet of dreams

A little boy sittin in his bed

saying goodnight to his mom and his dad

thinking of the things he knew he could do

on morrow's day when everything was new


But before he cast his fly into sleep

before his eyes slip into the tides

he scours the shadows where monsters hide

God's of watery dreams


But before his eyes fall into the sand

a nightmare emerges in the form of a man

a flowing specter to haunt a mind

to creep forth grins and crack the bell of time


Black bowler hats & cracked wicked teeth

evil thoughts & jangling jackets of tweed

walking in the closet of dreams

Feet fall closer, shufflin in

the touch of his breath, the depth of his sin

walking in the closet of dreams


Split eyes of flame, skin of a snake

may we die before we wake

the promise of a lie is what we'll take

walking in the closet of dreams


but before we cast our fly into sleep

before our eyes slip into the tides

we scour the shadows where monsters hide

gods of watery dreams


but before our eyes fall into the sand

a nightmare emerges in the form of a man

a flowing specter to haunt our mind

to creep forth grins & crack the bell of time


black bowler hats & cracked wicked teeth

evil thoughts & jangling jackets of tweed

walking in the closet of dreams

feet fall closer, shufflin in

the touch of his breath, the depth of his sin

walking in the closet of dreams


split eyes of flame, skin of a snake

may we die before we wake

the promise of a lie is what we'll take

walking in the closet of dreams

walking in the closet of dreams

walking in the closet of dreams

walking in the closet of dreams

## Torture meets Travesty

I smile slowly, purposefully
I have walked through a thousand hells
A thousand heavens dressed up in scantily laced attire

I have survived these horrors, yes,
Though not unscathed
Bruises left on body and mind both
Self created torture

I wear my scars proud though
Memories justified in pain
Journeys taken under the falling rain

I look back at my life
Sidewalks left in ruin
Righteous paths covered over in bristled thorns
Romances which choked and finished
Before even there birth had begun
Sorrow honeysuckled on ashes of guilt
Child wars fought through castles turned to silt

But these trials I speak of have made me strong
Strong enough to risk the gallows
Brave enough to learn the lessons
Though they caused my hair to bleed gray
And my eyes to crease over in weariness folded with wrinkles
Still, I cherish the wisdom gained through the revelations

While I today, I laugh loudly, insanely
Though noone listens or speaks
I howl in madness and ecstasy
Yet noone hears or feels

But the real tease to my queried thought
Is if this tickling, trembling sensation
I experience
Is it what they refer to when they say artists
Find inspiration only through loneliness

Isolation
Hopeless desperation
Delusions of glory stacked on top
Of mazes made of brittle glass
And if this is the truth of their reality
And if it is for this I am condemned
Then let it be so
For I will not leave what to me
Appears a tranquil garden
I will not forsake the tender touch of the flowers
I find here

So forgive me if I continue to blanket myself
In these insecurities written in child chalk
They refer to timeless memorials of sweet tears
I have walked

So please bear with me as I journey
Onward in this travesty mock marked
For I will do so until
My corpse unspeaks riddles
From it's half rotten tongue
I will push forward my mud sucked footsteps
Past the beasts who would tear flesh
Ignorant to the undead
Who would seek to spoil my livelihood and spirit

I will go on till I have reached the gateways
To Babylon itself
And there, there
I shall smile
Smile
Till my teeth decay into dust
Till my bones crumble from rust
Till I blindly and mutely stare
Into the death tapered doorways
Of illegitimate lust

Then I will demand
To be let out of Babylon
Given a chance to find my Avalon
Unmolested, unhindered

Then I shall trust
All those who come to my door
Then I shall share my warmth

**Stories**
**And dance with a wildness**
**Born of naked youth**

**And that's when I'll know**
**When my grave comes for me**
**And open's it's arm for hollow embrace**
**I will know I have left having**
**Eaten the forbidden fruit**
**And suckored on it's savory taste**

**And I will leave this tragedy make mockery**
**Of a life knowing**
**I was free**
**Then I will**
**smile**

# Lonely

I'm feeling lonely on a lonely day

I'm feeling lonely on a lonely night

I met some girls, they seem so nice

but when you get to know them

their heart's as cold as ice


Lon lon lonely days

Lon lon lonely nights

Lon lon lonely days

Lon lon lonely nights


I want to tear out my eyes

see what's underneath

spirit licking heart

or just rotting teeth


Lon lon lonely days

Lon lon lonely nights

Lon lon lonely days

Lon lon lonely nights

I want to climb

find myself alone

I want to fall

I want to break bones


Lon lon lonely days

Lon lon lonely nights

Lon lon lonely days

Lon lon lonely nights


I want to get high

brush feathers across my face

I want to hide

for once in my life feel safe


Lon lon lonely days

Lon lon lonely nights

Lon lon lonely days

Lon lon lonely nights

I'm feeling lonely on a lonely day

I'm feeling lonely on a lonely night

I met some girls, they seem so nice

but when you get to know them

their heart's as cold as ice


Lon lon lonely days

Lon lon lonely nights

Lon lon lonely days

Lon lon lonely nights


God Help Me!!

God Save Me!!!

I don't want to be alone!!!

I don't want to be alone!!!!

# River Rat Blues

There's some sailors on the water front
Who'll show you some gold
There's some girls in the whorehouse
With stories untold
But there's a special place you have to go
It's called by the name of the River Rat Show

There's gamblers and bankers and lawyers around
There's mayors, presidents and corporate hounds

'Cause there's rats in the river
Swimming against the stream
There's rats in the river
And it's all a fucking dream

You'll see mysteries, fantasies and
Willful woeful stories
Sex shows, coke blows
And whipping, spanking frenzies

And this is a god damn ugly scene
But it is a dream of reality
It's dirty and smelly and
Downright slutty
It's crazed and mad
It's a type of leprosy

'Cause there's rats in the river
Swimming against the stream
There's rats in the river
And it's all a fucking dream

There's some sailors on the waterfront
Who'll show you some gold
There's some girls in the whorehouse
With stories untold
But there's a special place
You have to go
It's called by the name of the River Rat Show

Rats in the rivers
Rivers and the rats

95

# The Television King

## I want to be the Television King

Get a little bit of everything
Gonna be a real big star
Drive through the streets
In a show doll car
Get my name written in tar
Lose my soul in a private dancer bar

'Cause then I'll be on M.T.V.
'Cause then I'll be the T.V. King
everybody will know me
I'll be in the movies
I'll be rich and famous
No longer poor and shameless

They'll be women around
Dreaming and drinking in mazelike towns
Clowns with frowns

I'm the T.V. King
Don't need no Queen
I'm the T.V. King
Wanna hear the church bells ring
They go ding a ling a ling

'Cause now I am the Television King
got a little bit of everything
got my own show on fucking M.T.V.
go figure

# Everybody has an off day

Death rounds hollow eyes
Contrition & compromise
Fleshly it's advance
Stalwart it's determination

A lonely boy beggars
on a lonely street
In a lonely town on a lonely day

Lights from corner lamps flicker
Shadows on crumbling walls
While somewhere a woman
Cries for a child lost in dream,
In the inability to touch.
Concrete, man skulks in
Back alley streets tapping Fingers on murals trying
To figure out the rhythm of life.
Old Ghetto Joe Strums blues & croons about
The way it used to be....

Lines form & rustle in a rush to
Trade blood for food or for just
Enough money to needle their way
Through another day

While brokers, lawyers, politicians finger money
Till shades of green permeate skin while
Somewhere in a desert a soldier clasps
Hands to stomach stuffing entrails in
The hopes of prolonging a foregone conclusion
Sadness has a certain appeal when faced with joy

Somewhere a child breaks his toys
Parents watching as they fuck
Smoking joints through slips of lips
Tips of candles wavering flames for a celebration
Of religion while priests fondle young boys
Explaining to them the merits of celibacy
How right it is when faced with temptation

Motel rooms flash neon
Wanderers searching for the
Reality of God
While teenage girls rubbing swollen bellies
Wait for the next trick to pick
And TV's keep losing the picture....
Perfection is as inevitable as death

# Walking away

I enjoy my time with her

but every time I walk away

I do so with cuts

bruised flesh

wrinkles where was once smooth skin

# Automate revolution

Now here's a story

short & sweet

about a girl & a boy

of course they meet


It's like slick thick oil

on a vinegar pond

like hot sex sugar

in the morning dawn


It's like a rooster race

with a one eyed jack

it's like a crack house condo

on the coasts of Iraq


Like dreams & sand

shaking the land

creeping in my eyes

like a rocking band

like a rocking band

I'm losing my mind mind

I'm tasting her sweat

I'm springing like a candle

in the deepest night wet


'Cause we are the Tin Soldiers

Automates in the revolution

Corporation

Annihilation


we are the Tin Soldiers

Automates in the revolution

Corporation

Annihilation


Now the story's done

like a sunset dream

and the corporate swine

are squealing for green

Cause we are the Tin Soldiers

Automates in the revolution

Corporation

Annihilation


we are the Tin Soldiers

Automates in the revolution

Corporation

Annihilation


So here's the story

from me to you

in a corporate world

where romance is...

where romance is...

where romance is...

No longer true....


Cause we are the Tin Soldiers

Automates in the revolution

Corporation

Annihilation

we are the Tin Soldiers

Automates in the revolution

Corporation

Annihilation


What revolution

what revolution

what revolution

we're still looking for the answers

to evolution

# To Sail the Seas of Broken Dreams(Poem)

There does it's mast blow
In the broken seas of shattered dreams
Where all things seem
A probability of impossibility
Where love drowns like a drunken sailor
Back washed in the storm of the sun's shade
Where all things made come undone
Where a little girl in the back
Of candlelit rooms
Huddles in the shadows of remorse,
Bruised and abused
In the memories of floating debris
Contemplative in the waiting of things that will never be
Where prayers crest and break
Upon the bars of cages buckling but never bending
Where groping hands of daddies
Rip innocence from the tender hearts
Of molestation's grime
Where husbands in drug dug daze
Beat submission with meated hands
Possession tattooed in a skin once smooth
Where even sacred maternal chains
Shuffle love like a chess piece in a game,
Like the backbone of a promise
Thrown as garbage in alleys
Where rats knaw the blood of sacrificial bliss
Where even a true kiss means nothing
Where all things lost become more so
Where even the sharpened sword of true love's bite
Cannot carve away the years
Where fear grips like an iron beast
Jagged teeth sunk to sorrowful soul
Where even the lure of another's
Pain licked eyes can not go
Can not compromise the eroding of time
Where the storm of broken hope blows
Where the letting go of breath
Waits for that which she will never find
Except maybe in the smile
Of Death's hollow promise

Shades of ghosts stealing away the day
Amidst a circle of flames
Where a man kneels weeping
For all that was lost
Blade of lowly means shattered in broken seas

Where a gleam in his eye holds the love of a dream

# Morpheus

This isn't your dream

your caged in your own nightmare

this isn't your dream

your caged in your own nightmare


Morpheus is walking on your soul

crumbling statues littering the road

Morpheus is walking on your soul

crumbling statues littering the road


You see what you want to see

golden bricks & mazelike dreams

little kids & sandbox greed

broken dolls & girls to kiss

bloody lips & lucid trips

moonlit thighs & tricks to lick


Morpheus, Morpheus

Morpheus, Morpheus

You see what you want to see
golden bricks & mazelike dreams
little kids & sandbox greed
broken dolls & girls to kiss
bloody lips & lucid trips
moonlit thighs & tricks to lick

This isn't your dream
your caged in your own nightmare
this isn't your dream
your caged in your own nightmare

Morpheus is walking on your soul
crumbling statues littering the road
Morpheus is walking on your soul
crumbling statues littering the road

You see what you want to see
golden bricks & mazelike dreams
little kids & sandbox greed
broken dolls & girls to kiss
bloody lips & lucid trips
moonlit thighs & tricks to lick

Morpheus, Morpheus

Morpheus, Morpheus


Let our breath leave our souls

the king of dreams show the road

lead us from this nightmare's toll

lead us from this nightmare's toll

lead us from this nightmare's toll

# Sunny times blue beat paths like a trumpet blowing heavenly tunes……..

I've got a pocket full of crumbs and barbed teeth with which to eat, the sunshine pressed against my back, a hand with four jokers and one jack.

I got missives climbing my back pocket like it's the yellow brick road, like a little kid picking his nose with a pocket full of toads.

I mean, I'm waiting for the jazz to tip my tongue, crawl along my teeth, hit the note that hungers me to eat, now my feet by themselves wander a straight line but when alleys swing blues it makes me move, croon, like some crazy street cat(Meowww!!!) Like that's where it's at, like a little bit of this and a little bit of that, two pinches of a hard horn blowing like a fat rat.

"cause you see,

I got a pocket full of crumbs and barbed teeth with which to eat, the sunshine pressed against my back, a hand with four jokers and one jack.

I mean I got dreams teasing lips, I got a hip that tends to sway, an eye that blows trumpets like a steel worker's hands, an ear that listens to the tap tap tap of drum stick jams, like counting ticks on the backbeat of time, being swayed by some internal rhyme, some drug dug rug ten feet high, Oh My!!!!

But you see, that's where it's at, some crazy street cat(Meowww) chasing love, love like it's the fattest rat, like it's all that, so I'm thinking I'm just gonna kick back, watch the sunrise and drink me a whole lotta wine!!!!!

# A Lollipop Garden

I got soul burn broken blues

I got a skirt in the peripheral of my crap shoot

and she, she, she.....


I got soul burn broken blues

I got a skirt in the peripheral of my crap shoot

and she, she, she.....


Hit the video


That's where the truth is

that's where the truth is

that's where it can be found

in this curvy shaking ground


That's where the truth is

that's where the truth is

that's where it can be found

in this curvy shaking ground

A lollipop garden in the sun

A lollipop garden in the sun

A lollipop garden in the sun

A lollipop garden in the sun


She's looking like a girl in a dress so fine

walking the lines in a garden of time

rolling her eyes like a web caught in the moon....

in the falling starlight

falling starlight

starlight....


hit the video


A lollipop garden in the sun

A lollipop garden in the sun

A lollipop garden in the sun

A lollipop garden in the sun


That's where the truth is

that's where the truth is

that's where it can be found

in this curvy shaking ground

That's where the truth is

that's where the truth is

that's where it can be found

in this curvy shaking ground


I got soul burn broken blues

I got a skirt in the peripheral of my crap shoot

and she, she, she.....

I got soul burn broken blues

I got a skirt in the peripheral of my crap shoot

and she, she, she.....

# The Journey of a Golden Hawk's Trial
### (One of the poems out of my first poetry book in 1995)

**I'm just here
And there's a thousand voices
A thousand histories
A thousand deaths and wars
Beckoning for my sight**

**Sovereign flags wave with no wind
As battle chants echo in the midst
Of strange lupine creatures
Howling in ecstasy and frustration
At the moon
Overbearing kings hiding as swans
Under the hammer of truth**

**I watch games of earnest
In which dice roll again and again
Always coming up seven in the end**

**Golden Hawk makes cameo appearance...**

**In the corner of a dimly lit club
Half shaven gamblers
Discard used aces for fresh jacks
Clouds conspire to strangle
The clarity of the map**

**Women and children die
Under a crying sun
Tattered remnants of society
Kneeling and praying
To scantily clothed statues
In what looks to be
A desert**

**Ghosts armed with teeth and worm rotted limbs
Circle and imitate what sounds like
Carnival frivolities**

**I listen and contemplate these strange things
As I stir the flames and cast a gaze
At the friends I have gathered for this story
Searchers of truth and glory**

The chosen few who hold their names wrapped in fame
Like the Liquid Gold Lion
False in his bravery and consolation
The Temptress in her slut fed
Deviltry and damnation
The Alluring Princess who smiles under the moon's radiance
Looking innocent but with a hunger for more

Then of course there's the Cackling Artist who cries with a grin
Strapped to a Jester with a bottle of gin
The Wolf who eats his porridge
The Leopard with his spotted repoitre
Not to mention the Priest and his Serpent
Full of remembrance and forbearance
Slathering and slavering for more

Princess smiles again, winks....

I shed a tear for all the pain that will follow
In my wake
Silver aura tinged Bard strums mandolin chords in blue
Blue
Wide sky window
Jump through

Time to start the hip shaking and thrust tucking
Throwing and showing
Wrinkled Wise Man
A dance of spears
Art of Zen
Dirt and tears
Innocent children

The voices quiet for a moment
Immersed in solitude
Stimulating the reasoning
For just being here

Scar Faced Peasant with dragons enmeshed
Along spirals in flesh
Motions to the hawks and herons
Lining the rhythms of fluidic thought
Curtains part

Another dream is sold in the market square
Pipe Smoking Priest bellows from his chair
Shows the price of the fare
Dust ridden ghost town

A wolves eyes glow yellow in the dark
Death imitates Dishonor
A coward's vision of glory trapped and enwrapped
In something that appears holy

I melt
Soft sand in a smooth mad sea
And I hear a call
Trumpets heralding the forsaken's twisted game
Cast under the swelling waves final moon driven journey
Into the Mother Earth's final thrust of desperation and depravity

Climax begins to brew....

Let's join hands and feast in our delight
Dancing and playing with the spraying
Droplets of rainbows and moonlight
Seven Hooded figures chant symbolistic runic riddles
From the space enfolded within the deep of twilight

The Devil asks for a candle lit date
Cloaked under laughter's mirth

The shadows unchain the Emperor and Empress
For their daily whipping frenzies
The Great Spirit's displeased gaze
Observes the exchange

Storyteller slips stealthily through.....

Did you know gypsy girls move best in flowing skirts
Their shapely thighs intimating the strength
Of their provocativness

Tight lipped nuns emulate and gesture in their
Disapproval
Blessed sister's dismayed disturbance
Is shaken off by the wolf who hides in the throat

I slip into the night hungry in my subservience
And independence as I prepare myself
For the hunt, the feast
Waving goodbye to the friends and foes alike
Who sweat and gorge in their complacencies
Lucky maybe

The forest's protective fold covers me
In it's solistic solemness
Real sultry
I shiver and squirm in my fright
And tongue drooling ecstasy
And I'm just here
Just here
And if you ask me
I'll shed a tear
For you
You
Just for being here
For it is a Golden Hawk's duty, burden and honor
Just for being born

Thorned Wreathed Thief grins,

Flipping a coin....

# Interrelating Balance......

....

All conceptual realities are just a different reflection of a universal visualization --
Essentially identical....

in the theory of participation by any one or more individuals and/or concepts.....

Differences express themselves only in the vocabulary used to articulate them.....

....

This precept theorizes that all realities, evident truths, are a single entity, concept,....

viewed at from a myriad of perceptions; be they mental, spiritual or physical....

in the alphabet of their communication.....

....

Again, all consciousness, interrelated, the vocabulary of understanding the only ....

differential---....

All evident perception harmonious, one --- Cause. Effect. Yin. Yang. Action.
Reaction. Sin. Grace. Death. Birth.  ....

One, an interrelating balance. ....

....

Thought ---....

From math to physics to philosophy to religion,....

all attempts to explain the same interweaving patterns of existence,....

the differentials only the vocabularies used to frame their intent, ....

and/or to assuage a particular perception.....

# Stalkers, Strippers & moms

### A Short Film

### By

### JD Glasscock

### All Rights Reserved 2005
### WGA REGISTERED

CUT IN::

1. EXT.  ALLEYS AND STREETS OF SEATTLE - NIGHT
MONTAGE
People shopping in nice areas.  Camera floats down alleys and streets of Seattle.
Homeless men begging for money, one kid, homeless, dancing coin across knuckles
next to old homeless man begging.  A street musician playing drums on plastic lids
seeking coins.

DISSOLVE TO:

2. EXT.  FRONT DOORWAY OF STRIP CLUB - NIGHT
Camera starts on front door and drifts through door into club.  Various men
precede him.

CUT TO:

## 3. INT. CLUB - NIGHT
ECU of burning cigarette then pull back revealing an old cowboy sitting at the bar
facing away from the dancers.  As camera pulls back revealing the cowboy, a dancer
on stage is dancing to music.  Camera also establishes interior of club.


(Played during montage, scs 1-3)

VOICE OVER

Where did it start?  What were the things that led
me to the roads, the avenues, the blood?  Can I blame it on
the abuse suffered by deranged mother's hands?
That would make it too easy I think.....or do
I take full responsibility for the choices I've made,
irrelevant to the past?
Now that, sounds too hard, too difficult to swallow.
Maybe it's a mixture, a little black, a little touch of
white,
and a whole hell of a lot of gray, abuse instilled in
an already dark heart.  I don't know the
answers, don't think I ever did, ever had
the chance.  But others will surely find them,
others will study my insanity, under a microscope,
under the guise of compassion and freedom,
somehow trying to understand the blood, the death,
the torture.  Haha!!!!  I wish they could of met my mom.
She would of taught them, she would of made them understand.
She would of shown them love.

## 4. INT. STRIP CLUB - NIGHT
Camera starts with an over the shoulder of Henry scrawling words into the
notebook.  We see what he is writing over his almost inaudible words....tick, tick,
mom, tick, mom, bitch, mom, tick.

HENRY

Tick, tick, mom, bitch, tick,
tick, mom, bitch

As Henry's scrawling and manic behavior gets more pronounced,, we see patrons
noting Henry's movements and begin to move away from him.  Two security guys

119

notice Henry and they start towards Henry's table just as announcer/dj speaks.

### ANNOUNCER

Ok, you cretins, put your grimy paws
together for the Queen of Lust, the
sultry, sensuous, Lilith, the star
and crème of all our lovely dancers.

Everyone's eyes focus on stage and Lilith, even Henry.  Henry stops writing and
looks up toward the stage and Lilith.  Stage fog surrounds the stage, and one leg lifts
through the fog.  Lilith begins her number and the camera surveys her body - her
lips, her eyes, her thighs, her breasts.  As her dance ends, we see Henry is back to
scribbling, a fevered gleam to his eye, whispering.

### HENRY

Tick, tick, mom, tick, Lilith,
beauty, tick, tick, hatred,
mom, bitch, Lilith, tick, tick

FADE OUT:::

FADE IN:::

### 5. INT. HENRY'S FAMILY'S HOUSE - NIGHT

Henry, age eight, is wrapped in sweat soaked clothes.  His mom is at the master
bedroom door.  They have arrived back a day early from a visit to Henry's
grandmother.  The Mother is screaming standing at the doorway of the master
bedroom where is Father is naked covered with sheet also wrapped around a
strange naked woman.  Henry is terrified at his mom's ferocity.

### MOM

Again, again you fucking animal!!!  You fucking fucking
beast,
god damn unfaithful man!!!!!  Get out!!!!

120

Get out!!!!!  Take your whore with you!!!
Never, never, come back, ever!!!!!!!

As Henry's Dad and the woman try to cover themselves and exit the place, Henry's mom grabs a yard stick out of a pantry and starts whacking both of them with it. Henry is terrified in the corner watching the whole thing play out.  Henry's dad takes most of the blows trying to shield his lady, his eyes casting furtive sorrow filled glances towards Henry.  He says goodbye with his eyes, then, walks out the door, his mom slamming it behind him.  She is furious, her eyes raging.  Her eyes come to rest on Henry's small frame.


### MOM

Your going to be like him some day, Henry,
a disgusting, unfaithful man, being led by your meat.  It's
in your blood,
who you are, a soulless man.  DO you hear me!!!!???
A fucking man!!!!!


Close up on windowed terror milking Henry's sad sorrowful eyes.  A tear licks his already char streaked face.  His mom's eyes soften for a moment, she embraces him in  a hug.

### MOM

It's ok Henry, it's ok baby boy.
I won't let it happen, I won't let you become
like all the other men.  I'll save you, Mommy
will save you.  Don't you worry.
I'll beat it out of you, that's what I'll do,
beat it out of you.  I owe you at least that,
at least that.  I'm your Mom,.....beat it out of you,
it's for the best.

Her hands are clasped in gentle loving repose as the words 'beat you' drift upon Henry's fragile form.


FADE OUT::::

FADE IN:::

## 6. INT. STRIP CLUB - NIGHT

Lilith is dancing on stage. Henry's eyes roving upon her flesh. Other patrons are
also enrapt with Lilith's body and movements. Camera worship's Lilith's
undulating form. Other patrons in club stare leeringly at her as she dances.

DISSOLVE TO:

## 7. INT. HENRY'S BEDROOM - NIGHT

Henry, now 18. He is looking through the pages of an old porno magazine. As he
gazes on the pics, his hand sliding up and down on his pants, his member. His
hands move faster and faster. His body leans back and his eyes flutter from ecstacy.

DISSOLVE TO:

## 8. EXT. HOT TUB - NIGHT

Henry's exotic dream finds him in a hot tub, bubbling and steaming, a coconut
drink in his hand with an umbrella. Two beautiful women approach the hot tub in
scantily clothed bikinis. They remove their tops as they approach into the hot tub,
their eyes running hungrily over Henry. They caress each other as the approach
Henry.

#### WOMAN 1

Oh Henry, thanks for inviting us over. We thought you were so cool, owning your own club, and this place, your own hot tub. Wow, a girl's dream.

#### HENRY

No problem ladies. I try to please. But no more wasting breath, join me, the water's fine.

#### WOMAN 2

We don't mind if we do.

They slide to each side of him, their hands reaching into the water to grasp his manhood as they squirm in ecstasy........

CRASH CUT TO:

#### 9. INT. HENRY'S BEDROOM - NIGHT
The door slams open in Mother horrific shouts, her greedy eyes taking in moments with tilt of head and grimace of mouth, the worn yardstick in her hands, her eyes lit up with the fires of hell. She slaps the yardstick in her hand.

#### MOM

Again!!! Ruled by your cock like every man that ever
drew breath!!!! I am sick and tired of having to teach
the same lesson!!! Is that it, do you want to be your
father, some worthless man ruled by what's between his
legs, faithful to no one, crushing the spirit of a woman's
love, fucking like a pig, like some disgusting
fucking man!!!! I thought
I had beat this out of you. I hoped
I had beat it out of you, last month, the month before, the
years before, but it just keeps going and going!!!! Maybe I
should just cut it off, save all the women it will ruin!!!

123

But no!!!!  NO!!!!
(Her eyes move to nurturing love)
Oh, I'm sorry baby ... you need more love!!!!!
That's it, it's not your fault, I failed....
I haven't done enough.
I promise I won't let you be like your father.
I won't let you be like all
the other pigs out there.
You know what has to happen,
don't you Henry?
Of course you do.


Henry startled, embarrassed and scared starts backing up into the room tripping over his pants that are down around his ankles.  He lands on the bed behind him. Mom walks up next to bed.  She looks down on Henry.  She raises the yardstick and brings it down hard on manhood, though shown using shadows.  Over and over again, Henry yelping.


FADE IN:::


### 10. INT. STRIP CLUB - NIGHT
Lilith just finished, now walking around tables while new girl gets up on stage and begins.  Henry watches her like a hawk.  He watches her talking to a suave, well dressed man, Henry's jealousy simmering.  Henry starts scribbling.  We see the words.  Sorrow, beauty, sorrow, beauty, sorrowful beauty.  Lilith takes a man to a back booth and starts doing a lap dance.  Henry watches lasciviously, checking to see if anyone notices.  His hand moves his rumpled notebook upon his member under the table.

FADE OUT:::


FADE IN:::


### 11. INT. STRIP CLUB LAP DANCE COUCH - NIGHT
Henry is envisioning himself as the person Lilith is giving a lap dance to.  She is thriving and jiving on his lap.  Then she morphs into his Mom doing strange

perverted mom dance, kinda funny.  Not really on him, more in silhouetted light
with returns to Henry's tortured face, then back to Lilith, then back to mom, then to
his girlfriend Eve, Henry's mouth whispering with longing.

HENRY

Eve...


CUT TO:


12. INT. BAR - NIGHT
Henry, now 21 is at bar, alone, nursing a beer.  The place is slow.  A very beautiful
girl is two seats down sporting a shiner, but still hot, also nursing a drink, looking as
if she needed it, the black eye looking a few days old.  She catches him looking at
her.

EVE
Alone too, huh.


Henry at first has to look around to make sure she's talking to him.


HENRY

Uh, yeah.  You too I see.  What happened?

He gestures to her eye.  She gets a little shy, but then a steel resolve floats to her
eyes.

EVE

An asshole boyfriend.  You think I would
of learned by now.  My dad used to do the
same thing, and then I go and choose a guy
exactly like him, fucking ass holes.
Sorry, you probably don't want to hear it.

Henry's eyes become deep pools, kindred pain.  He understands.  He moves next to
her and gently takes her hand, looking into her eyes.

HENRY

Believe me, out of all the people you could
be talking to, I completely understand, more
than you will ever know.

At first, him touching her, cause her to want to jerk her hand back, but looking into
his eyes, seeing the pain, she believes him, and is somehow comforted. Her hand
relaxes into his. Her eyes lock onto his.

EVE

I believe you do....(Whisper)

CUT TO:

13. INT. Henry's bedroom – Night
Henry and Eve enter Henry's bedroom, both looking nervous and their eyes and
ears roaming. Eve sits on the edge of the bed her eyes watching Henry hesitantly
shuffling through one of his drawers.

EVE

I thought you said your Mom
would get really pissed off
if she found a girl here?

Henry's hands stop searching for whatever hidden treasure that had captured his
spirit. His eyes took in Eve.

HENRY

She would... she would be a fucking volcano,
and shit I would get from it,
I can't even imagine, or wouldn't
want to...
I'm sorry Eve, truly sorry I can't...
I can't scream love to the heavens,

and yeah, a sight that would be huh?
But she wouldn't understand, would never
understand, not in one lifetime,
not in a thousand lifetimes.
But never mind her, she's at some new
knitting group she joined, a
group of women she can come home
and bitch to me about, ... never happy
if she has nothing to pull apart and
mutilate in her loving ways. (he sighs)
She'll be gone for at least a couple hours.
But that's not why I brought you.


Eve thought he might mean some romantic venture, her hand tailing her open
necked blouse along the swelling curves of her breast.

### EVE

So why did you bring me here my
   horrifically beautiful man?
Was it to depose me of my virginal bliss
(She laughs and makes a seductive pose)
   or depress me with the insanity
   and perverted ideas of you mom?


She makes a crazed face and claws with her hands but looks frightened when she
sees the pain in Henry's eyes, his hands renewing his vigorous search, clothes flying
all over the place. His hands come out with a photo, a glorious expression of victory
painting his face.

### HENRY

No, this is what I sought,
I wanted to find... to share with you,
   to hope you understood,
what I've never shared with anyone.
Damn, I don' t know why I even have it,
   after... after what he did,
   to my mom and me. Fuck!
My mom would slowly roast
   my testicles over an open
   flame if she knew...

Henry moves and sits next to Eve, hand trembling, hands the photo to Eve, then lays back, his legs over the bed.


HENRY

That's my father.  I know that he
left us, left me.  But even so,
I… I miss him, sometimes, when
the rain falls,
and I feel alone in the pattering
sound it makes,
when midnight has strolled past,
and the bruises ache from my mom's loving hands,
I take it out, and just stare at it,
imagine, dream, what it could have been
what it will never be
…Fuck, sorry.  You probably
don't understand, just think
I'm crazy, but it's the only
thing I can share with you, to show,
make me feel, that vacant
hollow in my heart…
that only that photo…sometimes fills,
that, well, you, (He sits up
and takes her hand,
staring into her eyes)…
uhh, I don't know how to say it,
sometimes, on some nights, when
street lamps flicker sorrow,
sometimes you step into that vacant hollow,
and well, I don't' know, I
guess I don't feel so alone.


His head tilts downcast waiting for the words crazy, and her leaving, goodbye, the word he knows better than all the rest.  But Eve's hand tilts his head back up, show hope in the soft caress of his cheek.

### EVE

Thank you Henry, thank you
so much for sharing this, for, for
opening up, for letting me fill
that, that place, cause you...you do that
for me, you make the bruises of
my father's hands...fade, lose,
lose themselves in memory,
in pasts that for moments...when
I'm with you, I can...I can dream they happened
to someone else.  Thank you,
thank you for that and for all the rest,
showing me, for once...in life,
that a man, can be, can be beautiful...

Their eyes meet, lock, their lips drifting closer, closer, till they touch ever so softly, then as moments pass, more urgently, Henry's hands sliding down her curves.  The door bursts open, both of them leaping up, Henry's mom with Hell's rage in her eyes, betrayal, shock.

### MOM

Al the pain, the lessons,
the memories of your fathers
devilish ways, and it stands for
nothing, cause here is his son
in all his father's glory...with
some wanton slut, some fucking imp!!
How dare you!!!!
How dare you!!!!  Get the fuck out of my
house you whore!!!!  You fucking
cunt!!!!  You will not undo all
that I have done, you will not make
Henry into his father, not while my fucking heart still

129

Beats!!!!  GET out!!!!
GET THE FUCK OUT!!!!


The mom grabs Eve by the hair dragging her dragging her off her son while Henry
stays immobile with shock and fear of his mom's burning eyes.  Eve try's to hold her
balance but is dragged out of the bedroom door.  Henry stays still, listening to Eve's
cries of his name, then silence as his mom gets her out the front door, then the slam
of the door, then the thunderous footsteps of his mom coming back.  His fear
shadowed his horror.  His Mom enters with her devil's stick of punishment in her
hand.

MOM

YOU WILL PAY HENRY!!!
BY GOD YOU WILL PAY!!!


14. EXT.  EVE'S MOM'S HOUSE - NIGHT
Henry, bruises on his face, a cut lip, now with Eve for six months sits on a bench
swing on the porch of Eve's Mom's house, Eve next to him, leaning into him, but her
voice passionate, her hands holding to him tight.


EVE

I can't believe all the things that
harpy you call a mom has done to you.
I mean, yea, my father was an asshole, but my mom
eventually got me out of there.  I don't know how
you've survived.  It's not
your fault your father was a two timing
bastard.  I'm sorry Henry, but your mom
is a psycho bitch.  And I don't know how you
defend her, that's the most maddening part of it all.


Henry, staring off into the night, takes a moment to encompass all that she says, his
body tightening into rigid stance as her words cut his mom.

HENRY

Cause she's always tried.  I mean I know she
shouldn't, shouldn't hurt me the way she does, but
she can't help it, she does it cause she loves me,
cause she cares, cause she doesn't want me
to be like my father, cause she doesn't want me to
hurt women, like you, like her, like my father's
always done, like your father's always done.

Eve gazes into his eyes, his dream, her hand caressing his face.

EVE

Your all wrong, so wrong, your mom has you
upside down and inside out, black is white
and white is black, your mind a fucking maze,
but I love you, I truly love you.

Henry holds her close, his eyes fidgeting towards unseen stars, cracked rainbows in
dreams never taking breath.

HENRY

(Whispers)
I love you too, I do,
just like my mom taught me.

Henry's eyes stare steel into the lens of movie magic, thee lens spiraling closer and
closer still, into the back drop of broken thoughts, deeper and deeper into his eyes.

FADE OUT:

FADE IN:

## 15. INT. WORLD OF IMAGINATION - TIME ANYWHERE, EVERYWHERE

Henry surrounded by dark shadows sits upon a throne. Scenes show around him, as afterthoughts, nightmares. These are the scenes. Medium close up of father's face and eyes then close up on eyes. Next, his father holding his mistress under a blanket of bones. A 8 year old Henry riding a bicycle down empty deserted street, except for a man slamming heroin in an alley. Henry's mom smoking a cigarette slamming worn yardstick against soiled palm...Close up of her face saying "Pig, pig, pig" followed by "beat, beat, beat you." Then his lover Eve saying "Black is white, white is black, broken down maze." At end he looks straight into camera from throne screaming "Insanity! Insanity! Insanity!" His hands holding his head his demons. He screams.

FADE OUT:::

FADE IN:::

## 16. INT STRIP CLUB - NIGHT

Camera comes out of Henry's eyes back into bar and dim strip club. He gazes into some nameless new dancer on stage and then leans down and starts writing. Lilith, Eve, Mom, Love, Sorrow, Hate, Pain, DEATH! Henry becomes rigid as Lilith comes from behind to sit on his lap her arm on his shoulder.

## LILITH

Hey sexy, you like my curves slip sliding this way and that, and even (wink)
Kink as you watched me on old Jim's
lap. So how about it, are you
ready for your turn in the shadows??? It's only twenty a dance,
forty if you want full service.


Henry's hands start shaking out of sight under table, crumpling his worn notepad.


## HENRY

Ahh, no, I couldn't, my mom, the stick, hurt.
It would be wrong, wrong, lust, pig, beat.

Lilith tries to catch all the things he mumbles softly. She slides her hand onto his
knee, leaning over so her breasts almost fall from fabric into view, her lips caressing
his ears as her hand slides up his lap.

## LILITH

Did you say your Mom hunny. No Worries,
your mom ain't here, and aren't you a little old
to be worrying about what she thinks anyways.
I promise, Lilith will take good care of you.
I'll make you shiverin' in all the right places,
you won't think of anything else. I am the best
at what I do, and what I do is please.

Henry's hands are now shaking with small isolated earthquakes, the pad of his
dreams and thoughts falling from his limp fingers to soiled decadent floors. He
squirms and shifts as her hand slides up his perfectly suited thigh, her lips licking
his ear as she talks, her breasts glistening in the soft muted light of lust filled havens.
A flash cuts across lens of pails of blood being flung from Henry's hand onto blank
canvas, only for a moment, a breath, before reality of the second again shifts into
focus and he finds himself up and walking, being led by trembling hand in Goddess
fingers towards back shuffled couch wrapped in dark shadows, same repository of
earlier Lilith movements on strange hips.
He is now shoveled onto couch, the music grinding, thumping, seductive and
irresolute, Lilith now moving, shifting, sliding onto his now bulging pants, her
heaven born ass now doing slow circles against his manhood, against the corruption
his mom has beat into his flesh.

133

LILITH

That's it hunny, let Lilith do her thing.
Wow you got a nice package going
on there, it's makin me hot.  So just lay back
and enjoy.  I'll make you forget about everything
except my hips on yours, no more moms,
no more loves, no more anything except the burning
in your pants.  It's what I do best.  So just relax and let
me take you for a ride.

## 17.  INT.  WORLD OF IMAGINATION - ANYTIME

This shot is flashed between Lilith Lap dance for only brief seconds.  It is just image
of mom with dark back drop.  She is holding yardstick slapping against palm, also
close ups of mouth speaking.

MOM

Beat it out of you, beat it out of you,
beat it out of you
You will not be like your father,
you will not be like your father,
you will not be like your father.

## 18. INT. STRIP CLUB - NIGHT

He is shaken by the memories and horrors of his mom.  He snaps and shoves Lilith
off him, her landing hard.  He throws money on the ground out of his pocket.  Lilith
is shocked, then angered as Henry mows across the club stopping to swoop his
notebook he had left at his table, the last word written large that the camera sees as
he heads out the door.  "Death!".

FADE OUT::

FADE IN::

## 19. INT LARGE WAREHOUSE - NIGHT

Henry in perfect suit and mirrored glasses holds pails of blood he is splashing across a large canvas. Shadows on the wall behind the canvas show half dismembered corpses hanging on ropes from ceiling. He starts smearing his hands over the blood he has hucked on the canvas. He talks, whispers, screams.

HENRY

For you mom...
For you mom.....
For you MOM!!!!!

CUT TO:::::::

## 20. EXT. ALLEYWAY OUTSIDE STRIP BAR - NIGHT

Henry sat still as moss in the shadows of an alleyway within sight of the back door to the strip club. Moments passed and Henry with mirrored glasses waited, breath riding upon breath. The door opens and Lilith steps out, now with long trench coat covering lustful flesh. A large aping security watches her walk away then retreats back into club, complacency now a doorstop to his routine of secure passage. Henry leans down further into the darkness. Lilith passes him fumbling for keys and one too many shots on duty, oblivious to fate winding itself into her path, soon, into her flesh. She glides down the darkened rat infested back street and Henry steps into her shadow. She makes a block south of club, just far enough for noise to do nothing but disturb rats and broken down dreams. Henry clasps her mouth, shoving her against dumpster hands groping, hurting.

HENRY

I love you mom, I love you.
(Tightens his hands to trembling mouth)
Be gentle muse, be gentle
and I will be gentle.
(Whispers in ear) If only
mom could see me, could see the art,

135

**could see the love.**

Lilith struggles, horror and fear leaping to limbs flailing, muffled screams and desperate struggles elicit back hands and spitting fists till Lilith is surrendered bruise, sacrificial lamb of tripping hope.  Henry peels her over dumpster his hands ripping shredded under garments, his own hands deftly lowering his pants, his hand shoving her head down and over, his other hoisting penetration, then hips finding rhythm against her now frail sobbing frame.  And as the movement of grinding hips starts thumping, Henry's eyes rotate and fall back to lids, his memory now dancing beats to the disjointed melodies of rape and abuse. The camera fades up into a full and bright moon.

FADE OUT:::::

FADE IN::::

## 21. INT. HENRY'S BEDROOM - NIGHT
This next scene is cut between the last scene.  Flashes of last scene keep interspersing for just a few seconds at a time.  Both scenes keep taking turns.  Henry is in his bed with Eve draped all over him.  He wakes without waking her.  His skin is seating and clammy.  He stands up and from beneath his pillow pulls a large knife.  This is Henry late 20's early thirties.  He pulls a crisp black note pad off corner table, and writes "It's time".  He exits his room unlocking three locks that are on the door.

## 22. INT.  MOM'S BEDROOM - NIGHT
This scene now alone, no more flashbacks to rape scene.  Henry is in Mom's bedroom coming towards out of the tilting shadows, his mom oblivious till the last breath when she looks up and sees the descending knife, in her bed, falling towards lullabies now turned horrific, her eyes wide as he last act shuttles into her only boy's eyes.

HENRY

Mom, just like you taught me.
You've been a bad girl.
But I love you.
(Swinging bloody arms, crimson splashing)

I love you!!!


Then Eve walks in on the macabre dance of Henry and his Mom.


EVE

Oh my GOD!!!!! What have
YOU DONE!!!!!!?????
WHAT HAVE YOU DONE
HENRY!!!!?????


Henry's glittering eyes filter back towards Eve's interruption of his master piece, but then his eyes dance inspiration, a final touch to a perfect world. He steers his dripping gore covered frame toward Eve, knife shining and wet. Eve starts back pedaling slamming over shoes on ground, landing on her back, still scuttling, now Henry towering over her, alien eyes in a once comforting setting.

EVE

Henry...no Henry, no
I love you, what are you doing?
Henry....Henry, HENRY!!!!


Henry's knife cascades down, blood squirting and squirming, shaping tormented pieces of art.

HENRY

It's all beautiful now Eve,
no more pain, no more hurt,
I wish you could join me, I really
do wish you could be here,
but it wasn't our time,
you had to go and keep mom
company....so she won't be alone,
so you won't be alone.
Now you both have someone to love,
forever. Forever and ever.

Flashes between this and that, come to a close, reality sets it's concrete boots.


CUT TO:::


## 23. INT.  HENRY'S MOM'S HOUSE, BATHROOM - NIGHT
This scene for the first few moments has flickering glimpses of Lilith and rape scene, shifting for seconds from this scene and the last before settling in the real reality of teenage warped imaginations.
Henry, nineteen, in bathtub, surrounded by the warmth of scented candles rimming the tub, strokes and splashes water in self implementing ecstacy. He has dreamt everything we have seen so far while masturbating. The door slams open, his Mom right on cue. He steps, his foul manhood fully erect in worship to his Mom's battered morality, his hand having slipped, from under a towel, his instrument of visions birthed. His mom starts to scream in anger, but now eyes blank movied screen, horror creeping in by inches.


**HENRY**

Mom, Sweet Mom.
I finally see, I am finally free,
I have finally understood what
you've tried to teach. I've had a vision
of stroking bruises and blues. I'm here to
give women peace, make sure
no man ever hurts them again. I will take the
love of mothers and sisters and lovers
and I will end their misery. I will give them sleep
and dreams that will rest their souls forever.
Just like you taught me.

Now come here Mom, closer,
you know what needs to happen,
let me show you love.


Henry's eyes dance into the darkening lens, blade coming down in bloodied story tale haunts.  It is time for his future to begin.


## THE END

CUT OUT:::


## VOICE OVER
Child abuse lasts a lifetime and affects far more people then you can ever imagine.

# Two tapping toe holds in the concrete of life

I'm here thinking about life
How it moves
Shakes like the grasp of death
In the last taste of breath
How glorious the moments are in the seconds
Eyes shift complexity of sequence
The parting of lips exhaling
The formation of goodbye
While the road winds
Through the foliage of concrete
The heat of the beat back sliding
Memories in juxtaposition of eternal enminity
Sound interwoven in the dreams of destiny

A testimony to the tilting of toes
Two tapping asphalt
The fault intrinsic in the creation of design
How everything is a pantomime of what's real
How the deal we're dealt
Falls short to Old Joe crossing the divide
How we realize only in the looking back
Of the fortune that rides our hips
The slip of beauty in the things we gaze above
How love lines the pockets of our histories
As we consume ourselves in the trivialities
Of our miseries

And to think I sup beer in toast to the pathetic
Posturing of my own inactivity as
The proclivity of poverty
Teaches me the myriad of possibility
No matter the improbability
A plethora of opportunity

While my fingers articulate the wisp
Of threads in the future cobblestones
Of our well nourished cognizance
As I sway to the circumstance
That stimulates me to the swallowing
Of thought
As my teeth creep sleep a smirk
For the answers unsoiled
In the worn lines of my palms

# Lumpy the Lazy Bear
A kid's book by JD Glasscock

On a sunny summer day in a beautiful forest glade the life of a lazy lazy bear was about to change forever.....

Lumpy was a lazy bear even to the normally lazy bear standards. He didn't like doing  anything that required him to move from the  comfortable ground.

Even eating, catching fish,  and sleeping amongst daisies in the summer field, required so much effort that Lumpy would not stir for hours afterward.

Now Lumpy being a lazy bear  had taken a cave near all the things  he needed, so he had more time, to you know, think about life.
 He lived in a beautiful spacey cavern down the path from the local stream where fish were plentiful and swam in lazy circles, lazy just like Lumpy.

 Well one week before the winter set on the fifth year of Lumpy's lazy but content life, out strolled,  walking towards the late fall stream,  the most beautiful graceful girl bear Lumpy had ever seen. Her coat was beautiful chest nut brown, and the way she walked, the way she swayed and swished those fuzzy paws, well, it stirred a hidden star within  Lumpy, beautiful melodies,  fading moonlit dances.

 But Lumpy thought to himself, to woo such a wonderful girl bear, whose name was Daffodil(His friend, Jeffrey the Blue Jay told him!), would require much more energy then the lazy Lumpy had ever spent on any day on any time in his entire life. He would have to catch fish for her, deal with the bothersome bees for some honey to impress her with his bravery.  He would have to walk and to run  and to play, no way, thought Lumpy.  Much too much work for a lazy bear,  he chuckled to himself.

 But day after day for a week straight he would see Daffodil stroll down the path in front of his wonderful cave to the stream.  It was much too

142

much to put upon the lazy Lumpy, to watch such a
beautiful girl bear walk the way she walked, the
swishing and swaying of her fuzzy paws. Lumpy
resigned himself to know, he was in love. No more
lazy days for Lumpy. A smile stretched across his
lazy bear face. He thought, for as much as he loved
laziness and the beauty of being lazy, his fluttering
Daffodil melodies, and need to walk and buzz past bees
for honey, catch fish, and bring a wonderful smile to
her beautiful fuzzy fun face were too much to be lazy
for.

 So he lifted his lazy lumpiness from the cozy
cave floor and did his own little swish to begin his
journey of wooing the girl bear of his dreams,
catching bees, and their beautiful honey, fish in
circling streams, and pick daisies for behind her
fuzzy ear. Lumpy soared on soft clouds, happy,
content, his dreams had come home, the stars shining
under fading moonlit dances.

\*\*\*\*\*

Now, year after year, when someone walks by the
stream, be it Jeffrey Blue Jay, Wendy the Warthog,
Frank the Frog, or Sugar Ray the Raccoon, they would
see what they always see, Lumpy and Daffodil strolling
and swishing and swaying and rolling and walking and
slipping the summer through winter through fall
through spring in love, and happiness, and only
sometimes, on certain days, laziness, for Lumpy, in
the end, was a lazy lazy bear.

# A girl flit flutters while I sputter obscenities checking my pockets for gold

My suicidal dives cross lines within a passage of time and yet still I walk , still I talk, still I breathe and it does seem a trifle slow, blow to blow, where is the golden joke I was promised, the eternal road to laughter.  I met a girl , she seems so nice, so still, but she tosses my frills like it's all a bout a game, name, I think friends was the word she used, but now abuse, I think that fits it better, storing away stolen tongues, drifting dreams for escape, how hate is such an easier thing then love.  I mean doesn't she see how when our eyes meet it makes our hearts beat, our knees shake, and our feet how they slide so smooth, like the way we shoot pool, so cool.  I mean we take out people like were mowing the lawn, taking out the trash, like the next hit is the next to last, and we roll and we roll and we roll till we say thanks to the next victim taking a stroll, but you see that's where I run the toll, my body stacking up coins like I got a free pass past death, like I'm sticking my tongue out and waving my hands, like saying "hey death come on over here and take me to your lands, I'm burned out here on dream's dreary sands."

I mean I got liquor flying down my gullet like it's the a-train, Like I'm on the next merry go round called insane, numbing the pain, cigarettes filling my lungs like it's the next rung, like it's the universal drug of compromise, yet still there she is again, those liquid eyes saying friends, friends, friends, till my thick skull hits the dead end, but then here we are trying to twist and bend, glide, cause this ain't the ride I bought a ticket for.  I mean doesn't she see how when our eyes meet it makes our hearts beat, our knees shake, and our feet, how they slide so smooth, like the way we shoot pool, so cool but I know, I know, I know, I'm the master of flunking school time rules, where all she does is flitter and flutter while I sputter obscenities checking my pockets for gold, for the next road to take me on out of here, cause I need a cigarette and one more beer, please!!

144

# Devils Walk Among us and God is Sublime

My Lord's works and words are my protection
his light, my guide

My Lord's works and words are my protection
his light, my guide

I move through devilish dreams
Innuendos with winks
Demons flitting across unclosed orbs
Circumstances veiled in memories
chitanous insect visage carved
In charcoal smoke
Oversized infant carryalls &
Child toy mobiles trailed
Across the furnaced veins
Of mirrored eye blinks in statuesque pose
Grass stains in youthful swings of bats


And I struggle to find myself
Restrain myself
Cajoled into the reenactment of
Abuse in the tongue of whips

A lady silhouetted  in red lace &
Creamy white curves paints
Broad strokes on the screen
Of a computer digitalized to sin
Then beckons with soft fragile fingers
Urging me to gaze upon her chiseled perfection

I avert my truncated trembling stare
Telling her no, I can't, your
Demoralized, demonized
Her sad mortal eyes
Tearfully torturously saying
"I know"
Me whispering comfort on breaths
Of air, butterfly thoughts
Her cool liquid soul burning in forever fires
Her battered demure lashes
lidding over glass stained
To look real

I will hold hope for you I exhale
I forgive you, I softly intone
My sharp tendrils being coerced upward
Ascending through carnival frivolities
And upside down worlds
Resembling my ass
Futures with no pasts
And I am shaken
Frightened
My mind whirling in madness
The roof of my mouth
Drenched in the sweat of sadness

And this is where I stumble, fumble
Into elegant ball room decadence
Ruby gowns & black-attired tux
Decorating people sliding & grinding
In social ass licking entanglement
People looking at me as a wild man
Raving lunacy, as if I was a man
In the midst of a self inflicted
Nightmare, me trying to talk,
But words sticking to teeth,
Emerging in slow mo
"IIIIII ammmmm dreeeeeeaming,
heeeeeelpppp meeeee!"

Bafflement, amusement & fright
Dancing across features perplexed
In understanding, frustration
Etched within my face

How do I escape a dream?
How do I slip back in the my
Well-worn flesh?
I start running, running
Away from these crazed make believe people
Gawking in ruby gowns & black tux,
Gawking as if I was the walking freak show
As if I was torn open fabric in space
And then there she is again
Tempting me with the snakes in her eyes

Lady of red lace & creamy white curves,
Her gaze boring into me
Drill precision
& the strangest words of all
Exiting her mouth
"Do you need a cab?"

I was shocked, confused, dismayed
Did this demon-coerced lady of dreams
Just ask me if I wanted a cab?
I couldn't believe it
Did she not understand?
Did she not see?
I didn't want a cab
I wanted out
I wanted to escape this
Raving road river raft of a nightmare
I wanted nothing but the surcease boredom
Of my pain ravaged flesh
But the words were immobile
Still sweetly sticking to teeth
Incapable of finding routes
Through thickened tongue
And just as I thought
My brain would collapse
My soul dwindled to tiny flickering flame
By this bizarre of worlds
This land of devils walking

I was touched, embraced
By gentle glowing hand
A martyr's deliverance
A lady of non-descript appearance
In gray maternal like dress
Soothing calmness cresting her flesh

Like angel radiance
Like burning sun
Breaths of wind forming reprievement
From her lips
"Are you ok? Can I help you?"
And as if that touch finally unglued the cage
I had found myself in
I scream, stumble over myself
Free & unfettered
No longer coalesced in sticky teeth
& thickened tongue
I lip the words
"I was asleep & now I am here"
Confusion crinkling my brow
Deathly fright in my fired eyes

And there she stood, all-knowing
Omniscient
That gentle touch the savior
Soft whispering intonations of freedom
"I know"
And in that instant of timeless love
I feel the presence of divinity
The warmth of God
And it is sublime
It is Heaven in clouds of silver
It is my ticket home

I sink feather smooth into
Welcomed tired flesh
Bedroom security
And my eyes snap open
Awake
Saved

My lord's works & words are my protection
His light, my guide

# Drug dealers secretly hide as chefs

**All drug dealers secretly hide as chefs**
I want you to know and understand this

I lived in Tacoma Washington once,
Worked as a waiter, became friends
With a chef, Hank was his name,
Biggest crack dealer in all of Tacoma
He called himself, though I
Only knew this later, much later,
After games of ball & drunken nights,
But that's when I understood,
Understood it all,
For that's when he took me the place
Of beginnings, births, drugs & sins, back rooms
Where infants sung tears & hunger,
Where grandmothers wait for
Death's smile to ride their hips,
Ease their pain, where teenage girls
Rub swollen bellies, smoke tarred hands
Drubbing walls covered in money
Shading towards red

And from there he ushered me to places
Of buying, consumption, hollowed out
Shells of buildings, shit pasted on
Floors & ceilings, broken sharp syringes
Left as toys for children,
Empty
Eyes licking lips in anticipation,
Forefingers tapping veins preparing
For immolation

And there I was, ghost circled
By shadows, mistaken for enforcer
Of payments, dues, only thing
That made sense, reason for white
Boys hanging in hoods creamed black,
White boys on wrong sides of tracks

And from there he cradled the tale
To where all tales start & finish,
Bar of sorrows, memories,

Where brothers pistol stuffed, sisters
Leather tough came to carve away guilts,
Lusts, addictions, where token white
Whores & one pale man stood as pillars
For whipping, and where my chef,
My friend concluded his fable with
Words drifting & dribbling off
Tongue thickened with conscience
Salivating through jagged teeth,
Relating to me how it is
On the streets, in the story,
In the blood, hard edged syllables,
Sounds forming toasts, confession,
Sanity and as in all toasts we
Lift spider cracked glass & drink &
Drink & continue drinking till the
Night slows, sways, falls
Till I weep
Till we all weep
Till dawn caresses us, massages us
In a lover's arms, whispers
Words & wounds taking us to
Homes & pillows, morals creeping upon
Us in dreams, nightmares about friends & hungers &
Seeds, about how in the wee hours
Of mornings & mists, chefs & drug dealers
Feed thirsts & desires that will
Never ever be fulfilled

# There's Skeletons in my Closet & Fruits on my Lips

Salty memories carve scars
Down cheeks
Caressing softly, gently
Lovingly

Eyes roving past broken concrete
Buildings condemned & crumbling
Flashbacks in past supplication

And as I walk these streets
In hard earned starvation
Thoughts flit across lids
Closed in half remembrance
And the story forms,
This is how it goes.

And as I turn the corner of dreams,
Salutations,
I see the old man I always see,
Rag starved skeletal frame,
Eyes glazed & powerful,
Gray strings of wise hair
His hand cleaving air,
Beckoning, urging
To follow
And I do follow like I always follow,
Night in, night out
Footsteps heavy like thunder
Unsure like a child's fragile movement,
Passing through earthly ruins,
Churches fallen & forsaken,
Bodies frozen within passages of time,
The jagged teeth of alleys
Swallowing histories,
A procession of crows on rooftops
Waiting, sensing our arrival,
Swooping down behind us in
Acrobatic wingtip feather tucks,
Symbolistic runes in wispy sprays of wind

And he talks to me,
Mad ravings of futures circling

In on themselves,
Pasts that haven't happened yet

And the old man flicks gestures to
Beliefs long dead,
Righteousness no longer viable,
Prescient insanity fortelling doom
In the sedated sparkle of eyes
Worn thin,
Moving, dragging aged body,
Filthy rags, bony frail legs,
Shuffling down roads less traveled,
Unadorned & atheistic,
Stopping to contemplate cemeteries
With ghosts dancing in soft silent segue,
Graveyards with crazed woolen laughter,
Oblivion in snapshots of black & white

My feet synchronized to his step,
Him moving like he's forgotten the dance,
Fumbling, stumbling always to
The same destination,
To a door framed in lunacy's cackle,
A door with a sign that says
"All morality ends here!"

And this is where the dreams gets
Really strange

This is where the old man turns to me, turns,
Head twisting, body immobile,
Like an owl, like somebody who doesn't know
What a spine can & cannot do,
His gray strings darkening to
Raven feathered locks,
His glazed sedated eyes melting
To furnaced flames,
Frail body tightening to
Mused youthful flesh,
Wrinkles to unblemished skin

And there he stands before me,
Now hip cat cool,
His words a mixture of blues & jazz
Surreal soliloquies
Burning liquid

And this is what he says
"We are all bastards in a world of flesh
and Death knows your name!"

His gaze tears into me jack hammer proud,
Then flicks forward, his steel grip
Peeling back cackled door
And I
Stumble through
And now the lights are red, blood bright,
Illuminating shifty seedy salvo,
Shelter of lust
And that's eyes glued to morphing mood,
Wall grinding wall,
Lewd leering clowns,
Flesh on flesh,
Corner floor funneling entanglement
Of limbs in salivating drooling
Mixtures of positions,
Moans & groans dribbling
Off fevered tongues

And with a little twist of head
Conflict confronts
With shaking sweating youths,
Eyes blazed,
Actors acting sweet rapture,
Injecting themselves with small silver streams
Of needles crawling across scabbed up vines of arms
While my tortured veins of sight covet closure,
Escape from drug dug yellow brick road,
Slow stopped by
Mad jazzed youth of furnace flames,
His feet flurry two stepping
To up tempo blues stroked by
Whiskey jigging brass blowers lacing
Shadows on chipped scuffed floor

And again my feet follow,
Blind man's bluff,
Bleary eyed sleuth of slavehood,
Chips freeing poker grins,
Tripping toes laying deuces in
Cigar style stove of smoke,
Twisting through enmeshed undulating flesh,
Straddling & sliding past sorrowful

153

Eyes, ghosts with fingers flicking futures
Up inflated elbow crooks

And here he is again, circling me,
Hoarding me to dust deaf hall,
Liquid movement, calling card called
Pry wrenching jacked up maw,
Jaw unhinged in terror
Loosening
Tightened teeth

And now the sounds draw out, fade
To some other morning, waking dreams of ash
Burnt out fires in glory

And he hammers me,
Pounds fresh nails to
Skin scraped suffering,
Walls hooded to neck back flesh,
And then smiles, the kinda smile
You see in horrors, the kind
That creeps forward in inches,
Hits with a bricked fist

Then it happens, happening,
Bones popping & contorting,
Sagging flesh puppeting itself into
Shrunken frame,
All hallow eyes glowing
Winter white,
Soft sane shift of summer,
Limbs circling tiny spirals
Now toddler touched,
Child cherished

And he exhales whispered intonations
"Sir, I know the way, follow me,
we'll find it together."
Innocence floods fuel filling battered bruised tank,
Tiny feet clicking,
Wandering munchkin merry dance

And now I hear the flute flowing
Melodious song,
Shadows gone,
Pan pipe doorway fog

And we did arrive, I was there,
Wide eyes, clouds, blue strewn bright,
Warm waving sun,
Child of white winter sight holding
Trembling nerve needled hand, fragile fingers,
Shows me morning mists in infancy,
Deep sloping pastures tipping emerald green
Tickling soles & souls of feet

And we fumble, stumble in remembered steps,
Shape shifting through dreams on
A star dust wave,
Down, down,
Hills melting valleys into dirt destined paths
Where he leads me, leaderless,
Now falling knee cap smacking
Stone ring of tired tinder,
Rejuvination waiting in small flames
Licking triggers
And his finger pointing push tough tongue of fire to face
"We are at the birth of cages, choices, mazes,
and this is where your road begins"

And with this simple sifting truth
The child of mirrors & memories opens smooth palms
And holds out
The knowledge of fruit

**Excerpt from Feature Film Script**

# Two Deeds Past a Dead Man's Corner + Dreams and the Burning of a Pistol

**A Feature Length Film**

**By**

**JD Glasscock**

## EXT. PARK, NEAR BEACH – EARLY AFTERNOON

A small boy sits in a sandbox wasting afternoons in spinning flight to the sun,
building castles with heavy concentrated effort, wrist flipping plastic shovel through
sand. A three year old in toddler heaven. His father gazes upon him but his face is
lost in the bright lapping light of sweltering summer heat. All that is truly seen is
knobby knees in short shorts.

FATHER
Ok son, keep practicing
your shoveling. I want a
full grown Castle by the
time I get back. I just
have to make a phone call.
I'll be back before you can
Tick tock past the moat.
And Auggy, if you need
Anything I'll be in the
car, right there.

The Father rustles the boy's head and points out their car only 50 yards away in the
adjacent parking lot. The boy looks up with solemn loving eyes towards the only
parent he had left. The only family in the whole wide world. The son reverts to his
needful shoveling, piling the sand to the side to build his fortress. The Father walks
his way to the car and enters the black Lincoln, windows tinted shade. The Boy
becomes lost as his hands sculpt the sand. A fortress starts forming, much to skilled
for a normal three year old toddler. His eyes, deep and translucent, gaze into the
fortress. He seems to hear the sounds of battle, the roar of war. The fortress half
compiled, his hands warping past, making walls, towers, drawbridge, the image of
fortress fading as the sounds of men fighting men grow. Reality shifts.

CUT TO...

INT. LARGE CASTLE – DAY

Men in middle age garb tarry to and fro through the throne room of a dusty castle, long swords in hand. The three year old Auggy sits upon a throne much too large for him and is draped upon by women with large breasts in low cut gowns. The young toddler sees lunch in every sway of their bosom. A man looking for some importance with sword sheathed at his side kneels to King Auggy. Battle sounds imminent, the clash of swords and the explosions of siege weapons pounding the walls.

SOLDIER

Milord the battle goes
against us. They are
battering us with their
siege weapons. They have
almost breached the gate.
We will need you with us
Milord to repel them.

The soldier looks expectantly at the three year old Auggy. One of the women pouts and thrusts her bosom towards Auggy.

WOMAN

But my Lord it is almost
feeding time.

Lord Auggy's eyes become giant saucers of mother milk hunger, the sweet succulent nourishment of all you children. But the castle swayed, the explosions became louder. The voices of the soldier saying "Lord we must battle" and the woman saying "But Lord, it's time for your feeding" start to fade as the walls of the Castle cave in by a giant boulder.

CUT TO...

**EXT PARK NEAR BEACH**

Auggy's eyes take in the piece of smoldering Lincoln crumbling make believe sand castles. His eyes rivet from burning chunk of metal to smoldering smoking pile of metal that was his Father's car. Auggy starts to tear and cry.

**AUGGY**
Daddy?! Daddy?!
DADDY!!!!!!!!!!!

The stretched anguish of Auggy's wide and scorched throat envelope the camera.

**CUT TO...**

**EXT. ORPHANAGE – LATE AFTERNOON**

Two men in black suits exit a black SUV in front of the Perrywinkle Orphanage. The sign says "Perrywinkle Orphanage, The Children of Tomorrow, Today, Half-Price on Asians this week." The two men silently and resolutely walk to the doors and enter. After a short amount of time, they exit with Auggy in their hands taking him to the SUV. Auggy looks demoralized and confused and fearful. The SUV pulls off and drives away.

**CUT TO...**

**EXT. MANSION – DAYTIME**

The SUV pulls up and the two men in black escort Auggy to the largest mansion ever seen, acres and acres of land, tennis courts and basketball courts off to the side in the distance. A large sign sits in front yard immaculately done, very ornate. It reads "The Winnabaker Estate – Building Toilets Since 1913". Two very well dressed preppy husband and wife emerge and meet the two men in black, a few words being exchanged though too low to be heard. They then are given Auggy and the two men in black return to the SUV and leave. The rich man leans down to Auggy and pats him on the head. They bring him into the mansion. Fades to black. Then across screen. "18 years later"

CUT TO...


INT. BATHROOM IN MANSION – LATE MORNING

Auggy now twenty one years of age looks at himself in a mirror trying to give
himself confidence. He is dressed very nerdy but like he's going to the beach.
Pokadot shorts, very bright, and loud. He is also shirtless and very pale and skinny.


                    AUGGY
            Ok Auggy, you're the man,
            your  gonna get yourself a
            woman today. C'mon, pump
                it up, pump it up.


He flexes for the mirror, though a lack of muscles is evident. He looks comical in his
attempts though he is oblivious to his own frailty. In his mind he was
Schwarzenegger in his coolness and frame.


                    AUGGY
            I will go up to the first
            beautiful woman I see and
            tell her, My name is
            Augustus Winnabaker and I'm
            the man you've been waiting
            for.  I know it will work.
            I know it, I know it, I
            know it.  For once in my
            life things are going to be
            smooth.  Confident.
            That's what the chickies
            like.  Alright.  Her we go.


Auggy pounds his chest as Tarzan for Jane. He grabs a towel and his backpack off
the cedar chest to the left of the sink and mirror. He exits the bathroom.

Cut to....

## INT. LIVING ROOM, MANSION – LATE MORNING

Auggy is trolling to the front door as his adoptive parents are in the living room. The mother, Willhemina Winnabaker, sits in a chair crocheting, the father, John Winnabaker, sits next to her with an end table between them, reading a financial magazine.

**AUGGY**
Hey Mom, Dad, I'm heading to the beach.

**DAD**
Fine son, have fun.

**MOM**
Yes, son, much fun.

Neither parent even looks up as they comment. Auggy knows it would take a nuclear strike to elicit anything more than a yawn from his stuffy wealthy adoptive parents. The only way either got going is if you talked to them about toilets. Their one true love. His father would spend hours upon the newest model of Winnabaker Toilet hitting the market. Auggy exited the door with a sigh. Nothing would ruin his day. He was going to the beach and he was going to score. He was 21 and had never had sex, never even had a girlfriend. It was his time, the Horns of Sex were blowing.

CUT TO....

## EXT. MANSION, INTERIOR, CAR – LATE MORNING

Auggy sat in a beat up Hyundai. He might have to live with his adoptive parents while he went to computer school and worked at the local bookstore, but he would not take their money. Since he turned 14 he bought his own clothes, even bought this car, though it had taken him till he was 18 to save the money to do so. He was his own man, and refused to take their wealth. At first they were puzzled but like all things with them had soon brushed it off as rebellious youth. The few dreams he had of his father, the energy he got within those dreams, he hoped, if his father still lived, he would have been proud. Independence, self reliance, these were the things Auggy somehow felt, deep in memories he couldn't remember, his father stood for. And he certainly wouldn't be taught by his gluttonous adoptive parents. Though truth be told, he couldn't remember much of his father, just knobby knees, ha ha, the knees. They told him his father had died in a car accident and that no other relatives were found. Thought they had let him keep the first name he had been given by his father. Augustus, though no one ever called him that, Auggy was his name. He looked in the rearview mirror, ready to float to the beach in the high of summer and smooth talk a beautiful woman in a skimpy bathing suit. He did note that nothing he ever did was smooth, more likely to be clumsy and awkward, but today was a new day, and time for a new Auggy.

AUGGY

Ok, here we go. Ladies, your dream boat is sailing.

Auggy puts the car in reverse and turns the car around to drive it down the long pathway to the massive gate that closed off the estate to the undesirables as his parents put it. As he approached he hit the button on the opener clipped to his sun visor. It started opening. The gatehouse was empty. Stan the security guard had the weekends off and normally his cousin Phil was on duty, but Auggy didn't see anyone as he drove through the gate and screamed in terror as a giant black SUV plowed through the front of his Hyundai, twisting the front around. Auggy couldn't believe what he saw next as a man in a black suit and dark shades in the passenger seat of the SUV stared right at Auggy, through him, then the SUV took off driving down the road as if they hadn't just demolished his car, nonchalantly and in no hurry. Auggy immediately got out and looked to the front of the car. It was not going anywhere. He couldn't believe it. Why did everything have to be like this for him? He muttered curses under his breath. Then he replayed in slow motion the crash again, his face rebounding in slow mo' being snapped back by the seat belt, his face almost comical as he slow played and drew out the screaming of "No!!!!!" by him, then suddenly returning to full action, the crash, the glaring of the Man in Black, with dark shades.

AUGGY

Dammit!!! Dammit!!!! Dammit!!! Why does this crap always happen to me?!!! Do you have it in for me or something? Does God get a laugh out of messing up Auggy Winnabaker's Day?!!!!! Well not today, I don't care, mangled car or no mangled car I am going to the beach and I am going to score. Do you hear me GOD?!!!!! Augustus Winnabaker is going to score!!!!!!!!!

Auggy kicks the front of his car but only succeeds in hurting his foot, hopping around on one leg in pain. He rips the bent mangled driver side door open and pulls out his backpack and towel. He starts walking his way defiantly down the road leaving his mangled car sitting in front of the gate to his house.


CUT TO....


EXT. BUS STOP – ALMOST NOON

Auggy sits at the bus stop, the only one on a road where rich people lived, and no one took the bus, only one route by the schedule on the pole. No one was seen, no one on the road. The bus pulls up, and he get's on.

INT. BUS – NOONTIME

Auggy steps onto the bus and as he does he looks upon the bus driver, and sees an old man, as old as old gets, small with very thick glasses on. It makes Auggy nervous as he turns to look at a completely empty bus, he hears the sounds of desert dust towns and ghosts walking graves. The Old man notices Auggy's gaze and the look of timid fright.


                    BUS DRIVER
            It's ok son, soon enough,
            once we hit the city on the
            way to the beach, there
            will be more people then
            you care to have on this
            bus. It'll be crammed like
            the sardines my Mrs. used
            to like, yep, when she was
            still walking the land of
            the living. She always did
            say I drove too fast, and
            God seeing for me to
            survive, uh hell, that's
            the way the cake bakes, huh
            youngster.


Auggy doesn't like the story, and he thought the man might be exaggerating how packed it gets if this be any measure.

                    AUGGY

Sure sire, no problem.  Do
you know how long it will
take to get to the beach?

The old man glittered his thick glasses up at Auggy and gave a "Harumph!"

BUS DRIVER
Well son, they don't say I
have a lead foot for
nothing.  Depending on our
travel through downtown,
maybe 30 minutes, could be
closer to 40.

AUGGY
Great, that means I'll get
to the beach by one thirty
at the latest.  Then the
chickies are mine.

The Old man gave him a, not in this life look.

BUS DRIVER
Sure son, sure.  Now hold
onto your britches, here we
go!

And with that the Bus Driver slammed his foot on the accelerator.  Auggy went
flying back slamming his head and turning upside down.  The Old Driver laughed
and looked back.

BUS DRIVER
Get the chickies.  Sure son,
sure.

CUT TO...

INT. BUS – DAYTIME.

Auggy's face is pressed against the glass of the bus. The bus is crammed to
overloading. Sitting next to Billy on the bench is a giant of a homeless man, the
most well fed homeless man in the world, smelling of three days of trash and months
of no bath. Auggy tries to breathe through his mouth. When the call for the beach
is rumbled out by the bus driver, Auggy literally crawls over, through and under
people to get off the bus, then finally emerges triumphant falling down the stairs
and landing on his face. The Old Bus Driver shakes his head in consternation at
how pathetic Auggy is. But all Auggy sees are his dreams unfolding.

> AUGGY
> At last. I'm here. Women,
> here I come, The Auggy Ocean
> cruise liner is open for
> business!!!!!!

CUT TO...

EXT. BEACH - EARLY AFTERNOON

Auggy had envisioned his first day at the beach a hundred different days, a hundred
different ways, and none of them included getting beat up. Yet here he was, in a
secluded part of the beach surrounded by the freaks from a circus and one old man
of 50ish wanting to clean his clock. On one side of him he had a giant of a man, tall
and wide shouldered, maybe 40 or so, with amputations from his forearms down on
both arms. He had a maniacal crazed look about him, then next to him a punk girl
with a Mohawk with a shirt that said lesbians rule the universe, then to the other
side that which might of got him in trouble if he was being honest with himself.
There was two tongue dripping girls in extremely skimpy bathing suits grasping at
each other, one blonde, one brunette, the brunette being the one he had eyes for.
The strange group formed a cannibalistic crowd wanting to see the old man rake his
fists in Auggy's direction. The old man was wearing beach pants, no shirt, and had
army tattoos on his arms.

> OLD MAN
> I know you were looking at
> my girl you scrawny piece
> of fish bait!!! No one
> looks at Ted's girl, no one.
> I'm gonna black and blue
> ya. Or better yet, carve a
> nice piece of that chicken
> frame!

Auggy's fear went to whole new levels as he saw the old man pull out the biggest knife he had ever seen, more like a small sword. Oh please, please let him not lose his life for looking at a girl. All he had wanted to do was score at least once in his life and now it looked like not even that dream would find fulfillment. Why hadn't his life ever gone right, at least once. Auggy figured one of the hot girls must be this Ted's girlfriend, though they seemed too young for such an old badger. He noticed though that the Old man had been looking behind Auggy when mentioning his girlfriend. The old man was now flipping and playing with his knife as if he had done so all his life

OLD MAN (TED)
Boy you look like your
about to piss yourself.
But never say good ole Ted
wasn't an honorable
bastard. It just happens I
got another knife. That
way everyone can say it was
a fair one. Now Matilda,
dear, throw the boy that
little ole' sticker you
been holding for me.

Auggy felt someone tap him on the shoulder. The hot girls must not be the girlfriend he had been referring to. He slowly turned around, and leaped back almost falling, but wary of the butcher knife and the old man wielding it, now behind him, so jumped back again and almost crossed himself like a pretzel. Before him stood the biggest, ugliest woman he had ever seen. She stood at least over six feet, wider almost then Auggy was tall, and enough paint on her face to redo his adoptive parent's mansion, and on top of it the audacity to be wearing skimpy clothes. He was so shocked at the sight of her he didn't realize at first she was trying to hand him a puny little knife, almost looked like a steak knife, though wasn't. The shock reverberated within him. This is what he was going to lose his life over, this, thing, masquerading as a woman. The old man thought he had been looking at her, flirting with her. His hand clasped on the small knife she was shoving into his fingers. He spun around to face the old man who was looking at him like a raw piece of meat.

AUGGY
Sir, I mean, ahh, Ted, I
promise you, I swear to, to
you. I wasn't looking at

your girlfriend.  I
wasn't, and I do not, not,
know how to fight much
less, use a knife.  I mean
you really don't want to, I
mean, cut me, do you?

TED
Boy, after what you just
said, I want to stick you
even more.  What, my
Matilda ain't good enough
for you.  God damn youth of
today.  Can't appreciate
the meat of a real woman.


Ted waves and winks at the beast behind him, Auggy turns and sees her actually
blush if it was truly her blushing through all that caked make up.  He had to get out
of this.  Auggy looked up as the old man lunged at him swiping with the knife.  The
crowd of freaks and hot girls cheered, actually cheered this maniac with a blade.
Auggy danced back and almost fell.  His hand dropped the little knife they had
given him.  He quickly grabbed it and stumbled back as Ted took another swipe at
him coming inches from Auggy's face.  He was gonna die.  He was gonna die.  He
looked down at the knife.  Something flashed within his brain, a memory unwoven
from forgetfulness.  A memory of a knife and his father.  What was it, what was it
he couldn't remember, then it flashed into his brain pan like a stroke of lightning
pealing thunder.

FADE OUT...


FADE IN...

INT. MARTIAL ARTS DOJO

A three year old Auggy in martial arts gear stood at attention looking up at the
shadowed face of his father, the father wearing a martial arts outfit as well but cut
off at the knees, his knobby knees sticking out.  The father pulls out a fighting short
blade and throws it at Auggy's three year old feet, it's point sticking in the dojo's
floor.

FATHER
OK Auggy, show Daddy that
you've learned what I
taught.  Show Daddy and

make me proud Auggy.  Daddy
believes in you

The three year old Auggy bows his head and gets in first stance, small toddler legs spread, concentration steeled in his limbs and eyes.  He crouches then does a triple front flip landing, rolling, and swooping the fighting blade into his hand.  He then flies through a series of complex knife fighting techniques.  He ends with a double back flip, landing, knife in a thrust position, then holding the position for a moment before coming back into first stance.  He throws the dagger at his father's feet, the point stuck in the ground.  Then after a moment of serious toddler face, he breaks into small infant giggles after good deed done.

FATHER
Oh, I'm so proud of ya son,
so proud, you do the
Octavious name with glory
wrapped to it's maw.

Auggy's eyes lock onto the bent over father knees, knobby knees like a comforting blanket.
DISSOLVE TO...

EXT. SECLUDED BEACH - MID AFTERNOON

Octavious, Octavious, Octavious, his last name, Auggy's real last name.  Augustus Octavious, wasn't that a Roman emperor?  But he remembered, for the first time he remembered.  He remembered something else as well.  He did know how to use a knife.  Or at least he used to.  The Old man was straddling low to the ground, swinging his knife back and forth as the freak crowd jeered and cheered and the two hot girls molested each other in excitement.  The old man spun at Auggy, but Auggy who had drifted into first stance blocked his knife arm, came in close and laid the small knife against Ted's throat.  Auggy looked straight into Ted's eyes.  The old man finally saw that the boy did have some fire.

OLD MAN
Ok boy, good job.  I knew
you had some grit in there
somewhere.  Now gently
lower the blade please.  I
believe you that you
weren't looking at my
lovely Matilda.

Auggy thought about it but then the nervous nerdy shy boy he had been all his life resurfaced and he shyly removed the blade as if he didn't know what came over him, shock riding his hips in confusing flashes of his childhood memory.

OLD MAN (TED)

Ok boy!!!! You've passed
the test, now it's time,
time to party!!!!!

The whole group starts to scream in excitement. The punk girl breaks out and
drags a cooler of beer over. They break out the Frisbees, football. Various shots of
beach activities and drinking, a lot of drinking. Auggy is corralled by the two hot
girls, whose names are Sumi and Violet, Sumi being the brunette, the one he
worshipped. They flickered his eyes to large saucer moons. The amputee's name
was Hendricks, or at least what he went by, the punk girl, Sherri, maybe now, he
would score. The sun drifted to falling dusk. Everyone gathered their things and
started heading out to the parking lot. As they entered the streets, Auggy flipped
looking at his watch, then pulling the bus schedule he grabbed earlier.

AUGGY
Oh man!!! I missed the last
bus. It left 20 minutes
ago! How am I gonna get
home! I refuse to call
my parents. And I don't have
the money to get a cab...!

SUMI
Well hey you can come over
and party with us. Violet
and I live right down the
street. The whole gang is
coming over to blow our
minds, and maybe, some
other fun....

Sumi's hand slides down the front of Violet's bathing suit. Auggy was mesmerized,
his thoughts drifting.

CUT TO...

EXT. SAUNA, PRIVATE, DAYTIME

Auggy is in a Jacuzzi, a bottle of champagne and drool coalescing corners of
mouths. Sumi and Violet are in front of him in skimpy two piece bathing suits. His
eyes are stuck on their heaving bosoms.

SUMI
Oh Auggy, our such a man,
a monster of sexual ecstasy
waiting to explode.

VIOLET
Oh yes Sumi, maybe we
should help him.

They both saunter towards Auggy removing their tops slowly, seductively. Auggy's
hands reach out towards Sumi's breasts. He is in nerd heaven his hand squeezing
his first pair of breasts.

FADE OUT...

FADE IN...

EXT. STREETS NEAR BEACH - LATE AFTERNOON

Auggy's eyes are half closed, his hands stretched as if he was feeling a woman's
breasts though clasping nothing but air. Everyone is looking at him strangely.
Sumi reaches over and grasps his wrist. Auggy is shocked out of sexual reverie.

SUMI
Are you ok cutey?

Sumi gives him a flirting look. His cheeks are red apples in the fading sunlight/

SUMI
You should come with us
Auggy. Hendricks loves to
gash his amputated arms and
create art with the blood.
It's a kick!!!!

FADE TO...

EXT. BEACH - NIGHT

Hendricks dances around a bonfire in tribal witch doctor outfit chanting while Sumi
and violet in provocative outfits slice his arms with big butcher knives. Hendricks
flings the blood around as he continues to dance and howl.

CUT TO...

EXT. ALLEYWAY OFF BEACH - LATE AFTERNOON/DUSK

Ted intercepts Auggy pulling him away from beautiful and luscious. Hendricks is off to the side rubbing numerous scars along his amputated limps licking his lips.

> TED
> Ahhh, blood art, sounds
> absolutely stimulating,
> though the boy has had a
> long day, what with the
> blade fight and so many,
> ahh, (he gazes at Sumi's
> and Violet's breasts) other
> attractions. I'll get you
> home boy, come with me.

Ted tugs on Auggy as Auggy moons over Sumi as they turn the corner out of sight, all the others taking up the blood art attraction.

> AUGGY
> But Ted, ahh, c'mon, those
> girls.....

Ted companionably pets Auggy on the back as they continue into a parking lot. Ted is walking with a blue bag.

> TED
> Ah c'mon kid. I know
> watching someone mutilate
> themselves while their
> slamming a shot of Irish
> Red sounds like a real
> creative moment, but enough
> excitement for one day for
> such a young strapping lad.
> Hey, you never did tell me
> who taught you how to use a
> knife like that? I would
> of figured you for a
> couldn't fight to save his
> life kinda guy, no offense
> kiddo, but you do have the
> nerdy thing pushing high
> and wide.

AUGGY
Well to be honest, ahh,
I've never been in a fight
in my entire life.  It was
just luck I guess.  (Evading
question)  Didn't you think
that girl Sumi was hot???
How long have you known
them?

As they we're talking Ted walked up to a black jeep wrangler and climbed through
the open bars sliding into the front seat.  It is in a parking lot of a grocery store.

TED
Known them, not long at
all, not even Matilda, just
met them last week, a wild
bunch, and Matilda, the
meat on that girl, hmm hmm....
Sumi, she's ok if you like
the skin and bones type.
And your first fight, I
doubt that, you moved with
training.  I served my country,
Vietnam boy, I
know the difference between
luck and skill, but that's
ok, I'll let it go.

AUGGY
Wow, nice car.  I always
liked jeep wranglers.  I own a Hyundai myself, only
thing I could afford.

Ted reaches down and peels the panel off the steering column.

TED
I thought your adoptive
parents were rich or
something, live up in the
hills.

Ted is hot wiring the car as he talks.  Auggy oblivious at first looking out at the
street then turns and sees what Ted is doing.

AUGGY

What are you doing Ted?
This isn't your car is it?
Are you really stealing
this car? I can't. Can't
be a part of this. I have
a clean record, I can't be
arrested. I can just
hitch hike or something,
call my parents.

Ted's gaze says everything that needs to be said.

TED
Just when I thought I was
seeing some growth, you up
and go back to the nerdy
boy with no back bone.
C'mon boy, you need to
loosen up, only one life to
live, so live it up. I'm
just borrowing the vehicle
and I promise to return it
to this very space after I
drop you off at home.

He sees Auggy wavering, unsure. Ted knows the kid just needs one last push.

TED
Girls like Sumi like guys
with an edge, not flimsy
wanna be's with no nerve.

Auggy's face takes on the look of nails. If that's what would get a girl like Sumi,
well then hell, Auggy had what it would take.

AUGGY
Ok, let's do it, but you
promise to bring the car
back after dropping me
off?!!

Ted looked him trying to stifle a grin. The wrangler pulled out of the parking lot
and started heading towards downtown to eventually head into the hills of rich
people and their mansions. he turned the radio to a rock station.

TED
Sure son, I'll bring it
back, promise.  So what did
you say you adoptive
parents did?  Oh yea, it
had something to do with
toilets didn't it?

Auggy still had nerves riding his veins being a participant in stealing a vehicle but
he nodded at Ted never the less.

AUGGY
Yea, Winnabaker Toilets.
They have been in business
since 1913, my father's
great great grandfather
started the business
building toilets for the
army.  I believe they still
have a major contract with
the military I believe,
though I never pay much
attention.  To tell you the
truth talking about toilets
bores the hell out of me.
It's all my father ever
talks about.  I mean I know
the family fortune is made
on toilets, but what is
there so interesting about
toilets?  I could never
understand it myself.

Ted was listening, but Auggy could tell something else was on his mind.  It surprised
Auggy now that he thought about it that Ted had only known Matilda or any of
them for only a week.  He attempted to cut Auggy for a girl he had only known for a
week and just as quickly dropped it.  In addition, he stole cars, and had been in the
military according to him.  This man was the strangest person he had ever known.

TED
Hey enough about toilets
and men who find pleasure
in mutilations and hot
women, and yes, even hot
women.  Take my bag boy on

the floor.

Auggy apprehensively lifted the bag off the ground.  It was heavier then it looked.

TED
That's it, open it.

Auggy opens the bag, reaches his hand in, and his face becomes shock, nervousness and trepidation all wrapped into his boyish features.  His hand comes out with an old 45 pistol, army issued.  Auggy's eyes took in the pistol while something nagged at his memory.

TED
Yep, that was the gun given
to me right out of boot camp
in '67.  It still shoots as
good as the day I got it.
Had to replace some parts a
few months ago as I had it
in storage while I, well,
while I was incommunicado
for some years.  It's my
most cherished possession.
What do you think there
boy?  A lot of firepower
there in your hands.

Auggy held the pistol like it was a snake writhing within his hand.

TED
It's not gonna bite you
boy.  Take a grip of it,
feel it's cold iron.  That
pistol has got the history
of blood and sacrifice
etched in it's metal and
more secrets then you could
ever know.  The way you
used that knife woulda
figured whoever taught you
woulda taught you to use a
pistol as well, but the way
your holding my beauty, it
looks like not.

AUGGY
Look, I told you before, it
was luck. I've never been
in a fight before, unless
you called getting beat up
regularly fighting. But
Ted, I'm thankful for the
ride home, but driving in
a, a stolen car just makes
me well, well nervous to be
honest.

Ted tilts sunglasses he had acquired, giving Auggy the "as if I believe you" look.

TED
Look here young lad, Auggy,
I still don't believe you
as far as the fighting,
well (takes another look)
Maybe about the getting
beat up, but somewhere,
sometime, someone's taught
you something. As far as
the stolen car (reaches over
and rustles Auggy's hair)
Don't worry so.....ooooops
spoke to soon I think.

Something stirred in Auggy's memory but then he heard the sirens, turned his head
and saw a cop car behind them. All his dreams of becoming a video game designer
were gone, his first time having sex had changed to a nightmare. An image of him
spiraling into a pit of hell, a swirling vortex of crimson blood painted hues,
swallowing him.

CUT TO....

INT. JAIL CELL - NIGHT

Auggy has his hands pressed against soiled cell bars  A large black man of steel abdomens, and towering size grips his shoulder with a lascivious leer.  Two other large men are behind him.  Auggy looks through the bars, and screams!!!!

CUT TO....

EXT. STREETS OF DOWNTOWN - DUSK

Auggy snapped out of his imagination and noticed Ted was speeding up, not slowing down.

> AUGGY
> All I wanted was to be a
> video game designer, my own
> man away from my family's
> money.  All I wanted was to
> get laid!!!!  Get laid!!!!
> Now, now I'm gonna be some
> squeeze for some
> Neanderthal named biff!!!
> Why does this always
> happen, why!!!  WHY!!!!
> WHY!!!!

Auggy was becoming crazed in a swirling jail house thoughts.  Ted's hand came up against his head in a swat.  The pain cleared Auggy's brain.

> TED
> Hey kiddo, loosen up...I
> am not gonna let you become
> someone's bitch my boy.
> Your too nice a kid.  Just
> buckle up cause we gonna
> give this copper the quick
> slip as I like to call it.

Auggy scrambled for his seat belt, his hands fumbling numerous times and failing again and again until exasperated Ted while swerving around corners evading spinning sirens reaches over and clicks the belt in place mumbling "you're a mess". Auggy's nervousness now cascaded in falling streams as Ted maneuvered the car as if he had been doing it all his life.  The car swerved and bucked down streets, through red lights, the cop car now joined by a second.  Still Ted put the Chevy to the levy and careened around streets until finally pulling a u-turn into an alley after just making a sharp turn the cops hadn't made yet. The alley was surrounded by tall buildings and the cop cars drove past after making the turn but not seeing that Ted had then made the u-turn into the alleyway. Ted leaned over and opened Auggy's door. As he did so he pulled out of his wallet a twenty dollar bill shoving it at Auggy.

TED

Ok Kid, this is where you
get off the ride. That
should be enough money to
get you a cab the rest of
the way. Though I need you
to do me a favor. I need
you to keep my gun for me
till tomorrow. Just in
case those cops run into me
again I can't be caught
with a firearm, especially
not that firearm.

Auggy looked down at the pistol that had been sitting in his lap the entire time. He gazed at it like a viper slithering along his pants.

AUGGY

But Ted, I mean, take the
pistol, I don't know. I
mean how will I get it back
to you?

Ted pushes Auggy out of the car. The sound of sirens again start escalating telling Auggy and Ted both that the cops were circling back realizing they had lost their prey.

TED

Don't worry about it boy.
Just head to the beach
again tomorrow and I will
find you. Just keep the
pistol safe and don't, I
mean it, don't show it to
anyone, and don't fire it!
Now got to get going before
those cops get any closer,
and remember Auggy, keep
building those sandcastles

>                    my boy, believe in
>                    yourself.

Sandcastles, what did he mean by that? It stirred a memory within his mind. But with that statement Ted burned rubber down the street leaving Auggy holding a pistol older then he was in his hand until he realized he was holding a pistol and quickly put it in his backpack his eyes darting here and there to make sure on one saw, but in the alley nothing and no one were around. He slipped his back pack back on and left to find a cab.

CUT TO...

INT. AUGGY'S HOUSE FOYER - EVENING

Auggy entered the house tired and confused and exhausted after the knife fight, stolen car, walking with a pistol in his back pack. His parents were in the same place they were when he left doing the same thing, his father reading a financial magazine and his mother crocheting.

>                    FATHER
>              Hello son, your car was
>                found in front of the
>              mansion, it has been taken
>              to the junkyard. A new car
>                shall be here by morning
>              for your use if needed. So
>                how was your day at the
>                    beach son?

>                    MOTHER
>            Yes son, how was your day?

All these words were issued while neither of their eyes had ever left of lifted to Auggy's face. His foster father still looked at the financial magazine, his foster mother, still crocheting. It was almost creepy, their behavior even strange for them.

>                    AUGGY
>            You won't even believe what
>            happened to me today. Not
>                even do I believe what
>            happened to me today. I
>              mean, it all started this
>              morning when two guys in
>              black suits and in an SUV
>            plowed through my car right
>              in front then kept driving

as if they hadn't just
almost killed me, then, I
took a bus down to the
beach which was a trial in
itself, then there was a
knife fight!!!! I almost
died but found miraculously
that somehow I know how to
wield a knife. Then there
were these beautiful women
and an old man, which was
the same guy that was
trying to kill me with a
knife, that was until like
I said, I found I could use
a knife, a memory of my
father, no really, actually
had a memory of my father,
then we ended up being
friends, hanging, having
fun, then I missed the bus,
and, and that same guy, his name is Ted, he said he
would give me a ride home,
but before I knew it, I
realized he had stolen the
car that he gave me a ride
home in, then cops were chasing us. I thought my
whole life was over, but
then he lost them and told
me to get out while he
returned the car, though I
don't know if I believe him
about that, and he gave me
money to take a cab home,
and here I am.

Auggy noticed after finishing that his parents had not responded at all. Their focus still on their respective activities. Now normally his adoptive parents were a little detached but this was strange even for them. He had just told home the strangest day he things anyone had ever had, and they hadn't eve responded.

AUGGY
Did you hear what I just
said??!!!!

# Concrete in the Faith of Salutations

Disconnected....detached vibratory ascertations in the climax of need....how long can one extend passion without the colusionary cementation of touch.....it is these thoughts playing merry go dutch in the cavernous vacuum of my fevered flesh...it is in the want...the hungering connection of lips to skin...the dream revolving on a spinning pirrouette of yearning fruition in the collapse of reality's teeth.....how can one hold to the stretching of limbs across the immensity of desert dividing that which one seeks and the totalitarian crumbling of hearts shattered upon scalding asphalt....let us contemplate the arena of faith....licking the pulpit of transcendence and belief with the most tenous of chains....love forged in the embrace that stands in ghostly salute..I tarry within this boxed off corridors of meandering flicks of empathic resolve......but in bones and cartoons of characature.....I tilt prayers to the shaking visions that what I hold is truth...and in it's rarity I shall taste the soverety of it's binding in and of itself in the meat of concrete....it must...for breath to continue to exit the pumping of my heaving lungs.....it must ...this story must color itself real.....otherwise my dissolution is inevitable.....

# Lonely is a word short on definition

This world is a mockery of hopes and dreams, yet still, hopes & dreams flicker
across the insides of lids, blinking and winking till reality fragments, coalesces into
pretty landscapes, beauty
grinding itself into thoughts, love shoving it's tongue
down eternity's throat, hips swaying in step to destiny's hope,
what a joke.

We walk through this life as if in a trance, a drug dug yellow brick dance
of pirouettes and stumbles off the stage

We stare stupid at suffering, insensitive to death's carnal grip, white bone skin
dripping skeletal visions, boxes of colors flying frames of pictures, antennas
discarding ideals and where to get the next meal,
stomachs bloating, starvation in the scraps we throw off platinum cards, credit
approval in the gluttony sticking to teeth, too full to eat, tongues lapping up misery
like it's a ticket to paradise, like the nectar of fruit, tasteless in it's sovereignty,
formless in the flesh falling tattered against burning asphalt.

I collect tears in broken bottles to remember the times I cried,
there are very few

I touch myself to make sure I'm real
then become sad when I realize I am

Sometimes I dream about flying, spreading wings against
gray tilted sky, seeing how close to the sun I can come

Sometimes I hope, hopeful that soon I will say goodbye, goodbye to
the hopelessness, dreamlessness, let it chew the fire trails
spitting off my spirit spinning into the void of non emotion, where though itself is a
dream, where death can make you scream,
like it's the first time.

Sometimes, the word, lonely, doesn't begin to encompass the feeling, sometimes,
nothing can.

## Hearts are broken skies in the emptiness of dreams

my heart is dust upon the heels of a woman's insanity....she carved into flesh the words of a story....a sad sad tale of deceit and manipulation......twisted folds of Hollywood glitz....she has broken me with sharp edged blades cloaked in love.....while the Fat Rats in Golden thrones laugh their glee and lick their lips in anticipation of her fall...their teeth sunk into the meat of her spirit counting the coins they rip from flailing limbs....and the one truth she holds to as lifeline....a mother's sacred chains of maternal care is the greatest of those finding satiation in the consumption of her morality and dwindling sense of worth....her creator chewing her divinity while spouting sweet words of comfort...her forked tongue lapping up the misery of her only daughter's dissolution....I am broken and the movie that is the back flip of this tragedy will not let go of my downward spinning breath.....will not release the demise of all that I dream....there is no pen stroke strong enough to elicit salvation in the crumbling bones of my death....no prayer that will surcease the cremation of my destitution....their sins and her nodding complicity in the madness of their schemes have utterly razed all that was held sacred and alcoved in divinity......the crumpled scrolls of fate have strolled into the horizon....and the weave has loomed into the maw of delusion.....love has descended into a 4 letter word congealed to disgust and deprave wanderings....it has shifted into a tool for bending heartfelt passion into something left by wayside docks and brothels with wanton cat calls.....the ambitions of riches and fame have outstripped the consoling croons of integrity....How have we fallen so low? My sadness is a sonnet of song echoing against the fabric of a non attentive audience shaded in worlds of make believe and fantasies playing marionettes with puppeteers savage in their pulling of strings.......my lover is folded in blood stained chains of maternal design and the abuse of a lifetime.....she was lost before her eyes registered the first inhale of breath...her limbs yearn for my outreach of gentle warmth as her mouth moves the words of hatred jacked into her veins by the replaying of greased up memories and laments whipping her into submissive inflection.....The saddest tale one can ever sleepwalk through is to watch their divinity rendered in shallow brushes of paint stroked by beasts who walk in cloaks shaped like men while your limbs are tied to stakes and the vision and personification of all you hold dear sinks beneath the waves....she is gone....and the wind blows over the empty sky.....

# Dead Ends and Dreams Begin

**I want to dig**
**Sink teeth into earth**


**Holding a heart smooth as infant skin**
**Watching as the scars begin**


**I'm strolling along river banks, hummin' blues to a silvery moon and tossing coins
to the smooth sounds of jazz on a back beat.**


### Fire Side Tales

**Thoughts....life....circles within avenues...a trip into an unknown road.....I am
happy...content...on my way to a merry go round dancing a jig.....dreams....a
fleshing journey of rooftops and blues...struggle and perseverance...sacrifice.....a
haven upon the hill.....lights flickering.... warming fires......... spirit ...a path in which
to travel and seek.....beautiful endeavor....a good measure to share moments ....
fascination... limbs spiraling back upon themselves.....churning
grounds.....crossroads...till weaves are played.....and strands settle themselves upon
fate's loom**

I'm flipping pancakes trip kicking a hackey while reciting Poe to a somber raven flitting through slits of lids

I'm imagining summer swelters with a cool blues flicking tunes at swamp rats dancing jigs in the bayou of dreams while toads ribbet about the ups & downs of life

I'm kicking small tomato cans against white walls hoping to create at least a modicum of artistic expression....the cat in the alley looks on doubtfully.

My bones are architecture of memory, adrift along the spine of history,looting the fabric of mystery,her legs wrapping my misery in constrictive longing

I'm meandering ghost halls jumping at creaking dustbowls and wandering paths into spiraling theories of unmitigated revelry.. limbs sparking history.memory.

My bones ache in withdrawal....shaking in convoluted and twisted roads...broken railroad tracks answering tumbleweed coyote screams..my eyes are painted visions

trippin' dueces in the hopes of singularity....holdin  odds....in the prayers of ambiguity.......let the forlorn whispers of adulating circumspect regulate the breathing of my ambutory neglect....and let the bones of my rolling wrist drop fate on it's uneven head....love is a backdrop of film noirs painting photos in the semblence of picasso visionary copulations......I have drawn heart laced intimacy at least once in this hop scotch runic riddle we call existence.. let that tributory title flick monumentous meaning to the breath drawn from the yearning of my heart in the blissful off balanced steps of my honorable yet truncated stutter steps in the honest laden tongue of my romantic persuasion....she is my heart....my dream in the fruition of souls bouncing truth...

**JD Glasscock**

liquidbard@yahoo.com
http://www.myspace.com/jdglasscock
http://www.youtube.com/jonathanglasscock

**Jd Glasscock's bio for writing**

.

## FILM --

**Short Films**

**Stalkers, Strippers & Moms -- Short Film(Dark Psychological Thriller)** The next child you hit might be the next person to kill someone you love. A dark drama about the repercussions of child abuse. At one point were 8 months in and three weeks away from production on this one when final investment fell through. Had Dan Dusek as Line Producer and King 5 showing interest in documenting.

**Prince Bumpernickle and his Midnight Foray** – A parody of a prince and his locked codpiece and his unfortunate run in with an amorous peasant.

**The Voracious Wolf and Three Degenerate Piggies** – a comical take on the wolf and three little pigs.

**Mr. McDougal's Big Day** –An old bothersome man shopping at the Magical Emporium and always getting the best of the salesman.

**To Sail the Seas of Broken Dreams**—A noble lady lamenting at her brother's grave.

**Not Enough Hours** -- half hour comedy script written on spec for the originator of the story line in Florida currently being shopped as a prospective sit-com.

**Feature films**

**Lost, The Legend of Billy Rockstar(Fantasy, Psychological Thriller, Horror)** – 140 page movie script, my first. Billy Rockstar finds his fame in conflict with his inner demons and the horror he was raised on, The Evil Man in Tweed.

**A Lollipop Garden** –  Feature Film (Comedy). A fantastical comedy about the treachery of lollipops.

A Nightmare in Wonderland – Feature Film(Fantasy, Dark Comedy). Alice is older and in leather and trying to kill the White Rabbit after getting tricked into the looking glass to save Wonderland.

Two Steps past a dead man's corner plus dreams and the burning of a pistol --- A crazy comedy about the abstract ,strange, and freaks of the world. A Feature film(Comedy).

The House at the End of the Road -- A feature film(Horror, thriller) about the last chance at redemption for the killers, murders, and rapists of the world in a house at the end of the road with two demons as a road block.

The Endless Road -- a feature film(horror,fantasy) about where the hopeless are bound, the demon infested world of the Endless Road. An old grandmother, orphaned child, morphine rock god, and teenage pregnant girl along with a few others must succeed in finding the hope they have forgotten or lose themselves amongst the thorn brushed hollows.

Laughter Echoes Empty to the Dead -- Feature Film(Horror). A sleepy port side town where a woman find's a history wrapped in old pirates, murder, and a demon that has never died nor left.

Kizz-Met -- Feature length film, romantic comedy about a shape shifting alien girl falling for an earth boy and trying to help him fulfill his dreams and in so doing maybe her own as well.

The Hawk, The Wolf & The Raven – Feature Film – Post apocalyptic story where corporations in the form of different cities have taken over what's left of the world. One man – The Raven – has been bio engineered to lead and unite all corporations, an evil despot, and been gifted through gene splicing with being able to see the future though only the far future. The Wolf is a boy raised too close to a radioactive hot spot and has been gifted with the ability to see the future though only the near future. The Hawk is the mysterious leader of the rebellion against the corporations and she helps protect the Wolf who the Raven seeks.

## VIDEO GAME DESIGN, DESIGN, THEATRICAL PLAYS & NOVELS

The Legend of Gaia – 10 book series on a twisted Arthurian Legend where Merlin is the son of Satan Bloodletter and they are on an alt Earth named Gaia where demons rule the world and 6 of the 7 great dragons that were given Gaia to protect are killed by the invading demon hordes and humanity has become slaves.  A legend says that only the child of a demon and a mortal will open the Gates of Heaven so Satan produces Merlin in the hopes of taking his demon hordes back to Heaven and accomplish what his ancestor could not, but Merlin, who is benevolent, rebels and creates the Knights of the Round to battle his father's machinations.

God'Riri'Roh – 200 page book on world of God'Riri'Roh.  From economics to history to city by city description as well as mythos and religion.

God'Riri'Roh' – The World of Blood – 140 page game design based on story of (RTS)

God'Riri'Roh' – Detailed outline on a seven part series of novels that the game is based on.

God'Riri'Roh' – 40 pages on part 2 of video game.  6 additional races "The Coming of the Jihan"

God'Riri'Roh' – 50 page design on role playing system for God'Riri'Roh'  Not finished.

Summer Sets on the Dead – 143 page novella introducing a duology continuing the story started in novella.  Duology entitled "Gods, Demons, and the Undead" Novella only 80 percent finished.

Lost, The Legend of Billy Rockstar – a 65 page theatrical play that the movie is based on.

The Children of the Apocalypse, Sorrow – a graphic novel series taking place after the final decimation of humanity.  Demons take over the world and make the remnants of society slaves.  The great spirits of the Earth choose avatars to fight for humanity's freedom.  20 pages in.

Lumpy the Lazy Bear -- Children's book, 1st book in a planned seven part series.

## POETRY & LYRICS

(Also played music for twelve years in bands, Sofa King and Shade & the Ocean Floor)

Seven, A Roll of the Dice – 50 page poetry book self published in 1995

Wonderland, a living nightmare – 50 page poetry book self published in 1996

Dogwood, a minstrel's tale – 50 page poetry book self published in 1997

Memoirs of a clown – 50 page poetry book self published in 1997

Lace and Grace – 50 page poetry book self published in 1998

Hallow is a dream – 50 page poetry book published by Inevitable Press, Pat Cohee, out of Laguna Beach, CA 1999

Flesh is a skein of itself – 50 page poetry book published by Far Star Fire Press out of Mission Viejo, CA 2000

Love in a letter – 50 page poetry book self published in 2000

Tree – 50 page poetry book self published in 2001

The Sorrow of Death at Sunrise – 50 page poetry book self published in 2003

Over 4000 units self sold of poetry books from 1995 to current.

Represented O.C., CA in 2000 Nationals for Slam Poetry, one of 58 cities nationwide represented.

Street Hymns to the Disconnected

www.ingramcontent.com/pod-product-compliance
Lightning Source LLC
Chambersburg PA
CBHW020906100426
42737CB00044B/389